D0335114

THE
COMPLETE
INTERNATIONAL
ONE-DISH MEAL
COOKBOOK

Also by Kay Shaw Nelson:

The Complete International Salad Book
Pasta: Plain & Fancy
The Magic of Mushroom Cookery
Yogurt: Good & Gourmet
The Eastern European Cookbook
Soups & Stews
The Best of Western European Cooking
The Delectable Vegetable
Mediterranean Cooking for Everyone

THE
COMPLETE
INTERNATIONAL
ONE-DISH MEAL
COOKBOOK

For Everyday
and Entertaining

Kay Shaw Nelson

STEIN AND DAY/*Publishers*/New York

First published in 1979
Copyright © 1979 by Kay Shaw Nelson
All rights reserved
Printed in the United States of America
Stein and Day/*Publishers*/Scarborough House
Briarcliff Manor, N.Y. 10510

Library of Congress Cataloging in Publication Data

Nelson, Kay Shaw.
   The complete international one-dish meal cookbook:
For everyday and entertaining.

   Includes index.
   1. Cookery, International. 2. Casserole cookery.
I. Title.
TX725.A1N43   641.8   79-65108
ISBN 0-8128-2675-2

For

OLLIE SWAN

With Affection and Thanks

Contents

Contents

Introduction

This book offers a comprehensive selection from the extensive repertoire of one-dish meals that has been created and developed throughout the world since ancient times.

The text and recipes pay tribute to the many and varied culinary creations which represent a wide range of appealing hot and cold entrees. New horizons for dishes varying from hearty sandwiches to exotic curries are explored. There are old-fashioned chowders and soups as well as cosmopolitan stews and ragouts. You'll enjoy the different versions of meat loaves, pizzas, and slow-cooking dishes. Innovative variations for such long-time favorites as pot roasts, meatballs, and substantial salads will intrigue both beginners and kitchen veterans.

One-dish meals vary not only in place of origin but in method of cooking, utensils, and ingredients. Some are simmered in a pot on top of the stove. A number of the specialties utilize a skillet or wok. Others are baked in oven-proof dishes. Some of the sandwiches and salads are prepared by combining cooked and/or raw foods.

It has been my good fortune to learn about one-dish cookery while living and traveling in various lands. I found a great number of fascinating dishes that form the basis of this cosmopolitan collection. Virtually every country has a wealth of excellent and interesting one-dish meals that have been evolved over the centuries by knowledgeable cooks using native ingredients and perpetuating national tastes and styles of cookery. Such creations have become essential to good home cooking.

Many of the recipes presented here are authentic duplications or adaptations of the regional dishes of foreign cuisines; others are my own versions or creations.

There are many advantages in preparing and presenting one-dish meals. Shopping for ingredients is easy since most items, except for a few foreign specialties, are readily available at local grocery stores. While the recipes call for a wide variety of food, I have emphasized less expensive or moderately priced meats, poultry, and seafoods. One-dish cookery can be economical and easy on the weekly food budget without loss of excellence.

There is no particular mystique about preparing and cooking any of the dishes in this book. All the recipe directions and methods of cookery are easy to follow. Preparation time may vary from several minutes to an hour or more, depending on the recipe. Nevertheless, all are well worth the time and effort spent in making them. With few exceptions, the work, including cooking, can be completed beforehand; and the finished product can either be kept in the refrigerator, or frozen if a longer period of storage is desired. It is easy to cook or reheat the dishes just prior to serving. Some dishes not only reheat beautifully but are actually improved by cooking in advance and reheating.

If you're a cook who likes to mingle with your guests when you're entertaining, or if you want to spend time with your family before the meal, you will particularly appreciate one-dish cookery. The dishes require little or no attention while cooking. Most of them do not suffer if they must rest a few minutes after cooking, and are easy to serve attractively and simply. Those made in cook-and-serve utensils can be brought from the stove to the table and served directly from the pot or pan in which they were cooked.

The one-dish recipe will usually constitute the entire meal, and you won't need much else on the menu. A few, however, may require the addition of a starch or vegetable. If desired, a first course—perhaps a salad with bread—and a simple dessert may be offered to round out the meal.

Much in demand by today's homemaker, cook, hostess or host, one-dish meals are excellent for all occasions. They can be served with pride either to family or guests, and generate an air of conviviality which will make the meal relaxed and pleasurable. The appointments may be as casual or as elegant as you wish. Fortunately, we have readily available a vast variety of pots, kettles, baking dishes, casseroles, or other utensils to facilitate cooking and serving.

Each kind or category of one-dish meal has been dealt with in depth in separate chapters. I have included pertinent historical and background data and helpful material on preparation and cooking, as well as suggestions as to the most suitable utensils. I have also indicated the type of meal for which a given dish should be appropriate, but this is a personal judgment only and should not be considered restrictive. It has not been easy to limit the selection of recipes, but I have attempted to present a representative compilation that will afford a fresh and inviting approach to this type of cookery.

Throughout the book, the text and recipes have been planned to provide fare that not only is appealing, but is an interesting variation on the usual culinary selections. In serving these dishes I hope you'll receive and relish the well-merited appreciation of those who are privileged to enjoy them.

THE
COMPLETE
INTERNATIONAL
ONE-DISH MEAL
COOKBOOK

Cold and
Hot Sandwiches

Creative homemade sandwiches, served cold or sizzling hot, open-faced or closed, make marvelous main dishes either for informal impromptu meals or more carefully planned occasions such as Sunday brunches, luncheons, light suppers, and late evening repasts. They are also just the thing for all sorts of outdoor dining.

The custom of placing food on a piece of bread, or between two chunks of bread, dates back to ancient times. Centuries ago laborers carried such fare to the fields for midday meals, and warriors relied on it for sustenance during long marches and battles.

In the Middle Ages, when most Europeans didn't own plates for each individual diner, a slab of bread was used as a sort of mat to keep the table clean. Diners covered the bread with cold food during the meal and ate the bread at the end of the meal, thus creating the open-faced sandwich.

The closed sandwich as we know it today evolved later. The

name derives from John Montagu, fourth Earl of Sandwich (1718–1792), who had cold roast beef put between two slices of bread and served to him at gaming tables in London so that he wouldn't have to interrupt his card playing.

Over the years a wide variety of sandwiches has been created around the world. In the Middle East people still roll rounds of unleavened bread around hot or cold foods such as skewered meats, or they put the meat in "pockets" of bread. Mexicans pile various foods on thin rounds of fried cornmeal breads. In the Orient diners enjoy sandwiches made of pancake-wrapped foods. In Russia yeast breads are baked with flavorful fillings. Scandinavians favor open-faced sandwiches made with a single slice of bread topped with attractively arranged foods.

Sandwiches are now more popular than ever. This is particularly true in the United States where the sandwich has virtually become an institution, and an estimated 300 million sandwiches are consumed daily. The variety is extraordinary. They are prepared with all sorts of bread, any number of fillings or toppings, and in a notable assortment of sizes and shapes. Some of them have become internationally known.

Early American sandwiches, however, were simple creations eaten primarily as snacks, such as brown bread, corn muffins, biscuits, or toasted bread with maple syrup, apple butter, cheeses, preserves, cold baked beans, or seafood.

Gradually homemakers found sandwiches handy for school and work lunch boxes and created a number of combinations featuring jellies, jams, peanut butter, hard-cooked eggs, cold meats, and various processed spreads. In some homes suppers or luncheons featured hot sandwiches prepared with cold meats or poultry and gravy; or toast covered with a cheese sauce.

The later evolution of American sandwiches involved many factors. Some were creations of pioneers moving westward. Others were adaptations of European favorites. Restaurant chefs, delicatessen owners, and winners of national contests all contributed to the repertoire. As a result practically all commercial eating places began featuring such sandwich favorites as the Reuben, Club, Western, and Monte Cristo.

With the advent of drive-ins, quick-lunch counters, and fast-food stands, the nation embarked on a sandwich binge, dining daily on such popular combinations as Heroes, Grinders, Submarines, Hoagies, Poor Boys, Sloppy Joes, Corn Dogs, Chili Dogs, and especially—the national favorites—hot dogs and hamburgers.

Paradoxically, the all-American hot dog had its beginnings in Europe, either Vienna, Austria, or Frankfurt, Germany, depending on which "history" you wish to believe. Immigrants brought the wiener, or frankfurter, to New York and it first became popular at Coney Island in the late 1800s. In some regions of the country, the frankfurter is still called a "Coney Island Red Hot."

The frankfurter in a roll, as it is now traditionally served, is believed to have originated by chance at a Saint Louis Exposition in the 1880s when a concessionaire ran out of the white gloves he was lending to customers to hold his hot frankfurters. He merely substituted warm rolls for the gloves.

The term "hot dog" was another fluke. Sportswriter and cartoonist T. A. "Tad" Dorgan, after observing the sale of frankfurters hawked as red hot "dachshunds" at the New York Polo Grounds about 1900, began developing a cartoon about them. Because he forgot how to spell dachshund, the cartoonist came up with the name "hot dog," which has become an accepted part of our language.

The hamburger also had foreign origins. The name derived from Germany's port city of Hamburg where it was served as a round of shredded raw meat (which we now call steak tartare). German immigrants in the late 1880s introduced cooked patties of ground beef, stretched with bread crumbs and seasonings, to fellow New Yorkers. But the hamburger served in a white bun was another phenomenon introduced at the 1904 Saint Louis

Exposition; and since then, served with or without relish, onions, catsup, or mustard, the sandwich has become so popular in North America that it is eaten by the billions each year.

Sandwiches prepared in the home should be carefully made with imagination and fine ingredients. Of prime importance is the foundation which, in most cases, should be a good firm bread. Fortunately there are many varieties such as wheat, bran, corn, graham, white, brown, rye, and pumpernickel. Also excellent for some types of sandwich are small loaves of French or Italian bread, pita bread, tortillas, or muffins.

Day-old bread is easier to spread and cut. Always use a serrated-edged or sharp knife when slicing or cutting sandwiches to prevent tearing the bread.

Sandwich breads are generally spread with butter or margarine, or perhaps dressings, to prevent the fillings from soaking into the bread.

Some sandwiches may be enhanced with a sauce, a colorful garnish, or such accompaniments as pickles, raw vegetables, or relishes.

Here are recipes for change-of-pace sandwiches that you will find appealing for many occasions. They are easy to make, convenient to serve, and require few accompaniments or implements. Furthermore, they are nutritious, attractive, and, above all, inexpensive.

Greek Lamb Gyro

This appealing Greek sandwich is traditionally made with well-seasoned lamb cooked on a slowly rotating vertical spit. As the outer surface of the meat browns, slivers of flavorful hot lamb are cut off and put in warm rounds of pita bread and topped with other foods. In Greek, *gyro* means round. Beef may be used as a substitute for the lamb, if desired. This is a good sandwich for an outdoor meal or weekend luncheon.

> *2 medium-sized onions, peeled*
> *2 medium-sized tomatoes, peeled*
> *⅓ cup olive or salad oil*
> *2 tablespoons wine vinegar*
> *Salt, pepper to taste*
> *6 rounds pita bread*
> *1½ pounds hot thinly sliced garlic-flavored roast lamb or*
>   *spiced beef, cut into strips*
> *2 cups shredded lettuce*
> *1 teaspoon dried oregano*

Cut onions from top to bottom into thin slices. Cut tomatoes from top to bottom into thin slices. Put into two small bowls and set aside. Combine oil, vinegar, salt, and pepper in a small bottle or bowl. Heat pita bread in a preheated 350° oven about 10 minutes, until warm. Fold each pita bread in half across the center. Fill each with some strips of cooked lamb or beef. Sprinkle with a little of the oil-vinegar mixture. Top with some shredded lettuce, sliced onions and tomatoes, and oregano. Sprinkle again with oil-vinegar mixture. Serve at once. Serves 6.

English Chicken Salad Sandwich

This attractive chicken salad sandwich which includes chopped raw vegetables and nuts, garnished with asparagus tips, is excellent for a ladies' luncheon.

> *2 cups diced cooked chicken*
> *½ cup chopped celery*

½ cup chopped green pepper
1 cup diced, peeled tomatoes
½ cup chopped walnuts
About ¾ cup mayonnaise or salad dressing
1 tablespoon fresh lemon juice
1 tablespoon curry powder
Salt, pepper to taste
6 large lettuce leaves, washed and dried
6 buttered slices white toast
1 cup cold cooked asparagus tips

Combine chicken, celery, green pepper, tomatoes, and walnuts in a large bowl. Mix mayonnaise, lemon juice, curry powder, salt, and pepper. Add to chicken mixture; mix well. Refrigerate one hour or longer to blend flavors. To serve, place a lettuce leaf on each slice of toast. Top with chicken salad. Garnish with asparagus tips. Serves 6.

Provençal Pan Bagna

This flavorful French sandwich is also called *"pan bagnat"* or *"pain baigné."* The name means "bathed bread," as the bread is bathed in olive oil. An excellent sandwich for a picnic or an informal lunch.

6 hard-crusted French rolls or hero rolls
½ cup olive oil or mixture of olive oil and salad oil
3 medium-sized tomatoes, peeled and sliced
1 large red onion, peeled and sliced
1 can (2 ounces) flat anchovy fillets, drained
2 tablespoons red wine vinegar
2 cloves garlic, minced
Salt, pepper to taste

6 lettuce leaves, washed and dried
3 hard-cooked eggs, sliced
1 large green pepper, cleaned and cut into strips
12 pitted ripe olives, halved

Split rolls horizontally. Sprinkle cut sides of rolls with oil; let stand 10 minutes. Arrange tomato slices on bottom halves of rolls. Top with onion slices and anchovy fillets. Sprinkle with vinegar, garlic, salt, and pepper. Place lettuce leaves on top halves of rolls. Top with egg slices, pepper strips, and olive halves. Sprinkle with salt and pepper. Carefully place tops of rolls over bottoms; press down gently. For picnics wrap in foil or plastic. Serves 6.

West Coast Monte Cristo

This chicken, ham, and cheese sandwich originated in San Francisco and became popular throughout the West. Turkey may be used as a substitute for the chicken, if desired. This is a good luncheon sandwich.

12 slices firm white bread
About 6 tablespoons butter or margarine, softened
4 thin slices cooked white meat of chicken
About 4 teaspoons sharp prepared mustard
4 thin slices boiled or baked ham
4 thin slices Swiss cheese
3 eggs, slightly beaten
⅓ cup milk
¼ teaspoon salt
About ⅓ cup salad oil for frying

Spread one side of four slices of bread with a thin layer of butter or margarine. Top with a slice of chicken. Spread four more slices of bread with butter on one side and mustard on the other. Place, buttered sides down, over chicken. Cover with slices of ham and cheese. Butter remaining slices of bread and put, buttered sides down, over cheese. Press lightly with fingers and secure at corners with tooth picks. Using a sharp knife, trim crusts and filling to make edges even. Cut each sandwich diagonally into quarters. Combine eggs, milk, and salt in a shallow dish. Dip sandwich quarters on all sides into mixture. Fry in heated oil in a skillet until golden on all sides. Remove tooth picks and serve at once. Serves 4.

German Sausage-Sauerkraut Sandwich

Bratwurst or frankfurters in toasted rolls are topped with beer-flavored sauerkraut to make savory sandwiches for a supper or late evening meal.

> *1 medium-sized onion, peeled and minced*
> *1 tablespoon butter or salad oil*
> *1 can (1 pound) sauerkraut, drained*
> *2 tablespoons beer*
> *¼ teaspoon celery seed*
> *1 teaspoon salt*
> *¼ teaspoon pepper*
> *½ cup minced green pepper*
> *6 toasted frankfurter rolls*
> *6 teaspoons sharp prepared mustard*
> *6 hot cooked Bratwurst or frankfurters*

Sauté onion in heated butter or oil in a medium-sized saucepan until tender. Add sauerkraut and sauté, stirring with a fork, 5 minutes. Mix in beer, celery seed, salt, and pepper. Cook slowly, covered, 25 minutes. Add green pepper 5 minutes before cooking is finished. Spread toasted rolls with mustard. Put a Bratwurst or frankfurter in each roll. Spoon hot sauerkraut mixture over each. Serves 10.

Texas Chili Beef Sandwich

This popular American sandwich is always a favorite for a family supper or a children's get-together.

1 medium-sized onion, peeled and minced
1 tablespoon salad oil
1 pound ground beef
¾ cup catsup
1 tablespoon Worcestershire sauce
2 to 3 teaspoons chili powder
½ teaspoon dried oregano
1 teaspoon parsley flakes
1½ teaspoons salt
½ teaspoon pepper
4 hamburger rolls, split and toasted
1 cup shredded lettuce (optional)

Sauté onion in heated oil in a large skillet until tender. Add beef and cook, stirring with a fork, until redness disappears. Spoon off any fat. Stir in catsup, Worcestershire sauce, chili powder, oregano, parsley, salt, and pepper. Cook over medium heat, uncovered, 20 minutes. Spread mixture on bottom half of rolls. Top with shredded lettuce, if desired. Place top half of rolls over sandwiches. Serve hot. Serves 4.

Danish Smørrebrød

The Danish word *Smørrebrød* means buttered bread, but Denmark's national dish is an artistic open-faced sandwich that is made in infinite variety. Each slice of buttered bread has "something" on top, generally two or more ingredients with colorful garnishes. *Smørrebrød* is served throughout the day as a snack as well as for lunch and supper. When these sandwiches are eaten as a meal, the Danes serve a delightful assortment of them as individual courses. The first one is of fish, then one of meat, next a salad, and finally one of cheese. Each is served separately on a small plate or wooden board and is eaten with a knife and fork.

The preparation of *Smørrebrød* is an art and there are certain established methods for making it. First, the selection of bread. It must be of firm texture and thinly sliced. Crusty white, dark rye, pumpernickel, or sour rye may be used, but the Danes prefer thin, square slices of dark rye *(Rugbrød)*. The kind of bread used should complement the flavor of the topping. for example, spicy foods on white, and heavy combinations on firmer bread. Also important is a generous layer of butter, spread evenly and covering the entire slice. As noted previously, this keeps the bread from getting soggy and acts as a "seal" before the topping is added.

The choice of toppings may be simple or complex and may include fish, shellfish, meats, poultry, salted and smoked meat or fish, eggs, vegetables, salads, and cheese. Garnishes, placed over the toppings, include such foods as chopped aspic, raw vegetables, herbs, cold scrambled eggs, anchovy fillets, raw onion rings, pickles, mayonnaise, or sour cream.

Here are two marvelous recipes for *Smørrebrød*. They should be made as close to serving time as possible so they will be fresh.

Shrimp Smørrebrød

6 square slices dark rye bread
2 tablespoons butter, softened
6 lettuce leaves, washed and dried
3 cups small cooked or canned shrimp
6 thin cucumber slices
1 cup sour cream
1 tablespoon fresh lemon juice
½ teaspoon dried dillweed
Salt, pepper to taste
6 cherry tomatoes

Spread each bread square with butter. Top each with a lettuce leaf, shrimp arranged in rows, and a cucumber slice. Combine remaining ingredients, except tomatoes. Spoon a little over each sandwich. Garnish each with a tomato. Serves 6.

Roast Beef Smørrebrød

6 slices firm white bread
2 tablespoons butter, softened
6 leaves Bibb or Boston lettuce, washed and dried
12 thin slices roast beef
1 cup bottled or homemade Russian or Thousand Island
    dressing
12 onion rings

Spread each bread slice with butter. Cover each with a lettuce leaf and two slices of beef, folded over attractively. Spoon some dressing over each sandwich. Garnish with onion rings. Serves 6.

Knife and Fork London Broil Sandwich

This hearty hot sandwich, made with flank steak and mushrooms on a base of crusty French roll, is a good entrée for a company luncheon, light supper, or late evening meal. Serve with a knife and fork.

1 flank steak, about 2 pounds
⅓ cup olive or salad oil
3 tablespoons dry red wine or wine vinegar
3 tablespoons minced shallots or scallions
1 or 2 cloves garlic, crushed
1½ teaspoons salt
¼ teaspoon pepper
½ pound fresh mushrooms, cleaned and sliced
3 tablespoons butter or margarine
1 tablespoon fresh lemon juice
⅓ cup chopped fresh parsley
3 large crusty French rolls, split and toasted
About 2 tablespoons sharp prepared mustard

Remove any fat and outer membranes from steak. Put into a shallow dish; cover with oil, wine or vinegar, shallots or scallions, garlic, salt, and pepper. Leave to marinate 1 hour or longer, turning once or twice. When ready to serve, broil 3 or 4 inches from heat in a preheated broiler, allowing 5 to 8 minutes per side, the exact time depending on the steak size and desired degree of doneness. The steak is generally served medium rare with a juicy red interior. Cut across the grain into very thin, narrow pieces. While steak is cooking, sauté mushrooms in heated butter and lemon juice in a small skillet for 4 minutes; add parsley. To serve, spread each roll with mustard; top with steak pieces and mushrooms. Serve at once. Serves 6.

Mexican Tostadas

The Spanish word *tostada* means toast, but in Mexico the name refers to an open sandwich made with a fried cornmeal tortilla which is topped with several ingredients such as meats, cheese, vegetables, and garnishes. This version is prepared with tostada shells, available in packages in most groceries. The sandwich is good for a luncheon or supper.

1 pound ground beef
1 cup minced onions
1 can (7½ ounces) green chili sauce
1 can (6 ounces) tomato paste
1 cup water
6 tostada shells
1 can (1 pound, 4 ounces) refried beans, heated
2 cups shredded lettuce
2 cups shredded Cheddar cheese
1 large tomato, peeled and chopped
1 cup chopped black olives

Fry beef and onions in a medium-sized skillet until redness disappears. Spoon off any excess fat. Add chili sauce, tomato paste, and water. Cook slowly, uncovered, 12 minutes, stirring occasionally. Meanwhile, heat tostada shells in a 350° oven until crisp and golden, about 8 minutes. To assemble tostadas, spread each with a layer of hot refried beans and the beef mixture. Sprinkle each with lettuce and cheese. Top with tomatoes and olives. Serves 6.

Basque Omelet Sandwich

This is a good sandwich for a family weekend breakfast or brunch.

1 medium-sized onion, peeled and chopped
1 or 2 cloves garlic, crushed
3 tablespoons olive or salad oil or butter
1 large tomato, peeled and chopped
1 medium-sized green pepper, cleaned and chopped
½ teaspoon dried oregano or basil
1½ teaspoons salt
¼ teaspoon pepper
8 eggs, slightly beaten
2 tablespoons chopped fresh parsley
4 crusty white rolls, split and toasted

Sauté onion and garlic in heated oil in a large skillet until tender. Add tomato, green pepper, oregano or basil, salt, and pepper; sauté 3 minutes. Stir in eggs and parsley. Cook slowly, covered, until mixture is set and surface is dry when touched lightly. To serve, cut into four portions; place each on bottom roll; cover with top roll. Serves 4.

The Hero

This popular American sandwich is named "hero" because it requires a heroic appetite to finish the hearty combination. It is also called other names in various parts of the country—Hoagie, Grinder, Submarine, Torpedo, Bomber, and Zeppelin. The sandwich can be made with a wide selection of ingredients. This sandwich is good for a picnic or lunch.

2 loaves soft fresh Italian bread, about 12″ long
About 2 tablespoons sharp prepared mustard
12 thin slices pastrami or boiled ham
6 thin slices provolone, cut in halves crosswise
6 thin slices hard salami
2 medium-sized tomatoes, peeled, sliced and cut into
  halves
½ cup crumbled ricotta cheese
¼ cup chopped onions or pickled hot peppers
¼ teaspoon dried oregano or basil
Salt, pepper to taste
½ cup shredded lettuce

Split each loaf of bread lengthwise and spread cut sides with mustard. On each bottom half arrange slices of pastrami or ham, folded in half to fit the bread; slices of provolone; slices of salami, folded in half to fit the bread; and tomato slices. Sprinkle with ricotta, onions or peppers, seasonings, and lettuce. Carefully place top bread halves over bottoms; press down gently. Cut each crosswise into 4 pieces. Serves 4, allowing 2 for each person.

Beefsteak Tartare

In Europe and America an appealing open-faced sandwich is made with raw ground beef, raw egg yolks, and seasonings. It is served on pumpernickel, with garnishes. The name is believed to have derived from the Tartar practice of scraping and eating raw meat. The beef must be top quality and very fresh. If ground at home put through the grinder twice. Prepare the meat no more than 30 minutes before serving time. This is a good brunch or luncheon sandwich.

1 pound freshly ground lean beef sirloin
2 raw egg yolks
¼ cup minced onion
2 tablespoons chopped fresh parsley
2 teaspoons capers, drained
1 tablespoon Worcestershire sauce
1 tablespoon sharp prepared mustard
1½ teaspoons salt
¼ teaspoon pepper
4 slices pumpernickel, toasted
Garnishes: 1 medium-sized red onion, sliced and
  separated into rings; 1 tomato, cut into wedges; 8
  cucumber slices; 8 pickle slices

Combine beef with remaining ingredients, except pumpernickel and garnishes, in a large bowl. Divide into four portions; shape each into a patty. To serve, place each patty on a slice of pumpernickel toast on an individual small plate. Top with onion rings; surround with tomato wedges, cucumber and pickle slices. Serves 4.

The Reuben

This popular restaurant sandwich is now made in many versions. Generally the Reuben includes corned beef, Swiss cheese, and sauerkraut and is broiled or grilled. It is a good sandwich for supper or a late-evening meal.

16 slices pumpernickel or rye bread
About 3 tablespoons sharp prepared mustard
16 thin slices corned beef
1¼ cups drained sauerkraut

16 thin slices Swiss cheese
¾ cup bottled or homemade Russian dressing
Softened butter or margarine

Spread 8 of the bread slices with mustard. Top each with 2 slices corned beef, about 2 tablespoons sauerkraut, 2 slices cheese, and a spoonful of Russian dressing. Cover with remaining bread slices and press lightly. Spread outside surfaces with butter or margarine. Broil or grill slowly until cheese melts. Serve with dill pickles and potato chips, if desired. Serves 8.

Continental Mushroom-Bacon Sandwich

This attractive sandwich is flavored with dillweed and sour cream. Serve for a weekend luncheon or brunch.

1 pound fresh mushrooms, cleaned and sliced
¼ cup butter or margarine
2 tablespoons fresh lemon juice
2 tablespoons minced shallots or scallions
¾ teaspoon salt
⅛ teaspoon pepper
4 slices white bread, toasted
2 cups sour cream
1 teaspoon dillweed
8 strips bacon, fried crisp and halved
4 slices tomato, halved

Sauté mushrooms in heated butter and lemon juice in a large skillet 3 minutes. Add shallots or scallions; sauté 1 minute. Mix in salt and pepper. Spoon over toast slices, placed on a broiler tray. Top with sour cream and dillweed, previously combined, and bacon strips. Place under a preheated broiler 1 or 2 minutes. Serve at once on individual plates. Garnish with tomato slices. Serves 4.

Kentucky Hot Brown Sandwich

This chicken sandwich, a specialty of Louisville's Brown Hotel, is traditionally served at Kentucky Derby breakfasts. It is a good brunch or luncheon sandwich.

> *2 tablespoons butter or margarine*
> *1 tablespoon all-purpose flour*
> *1 cup light cream or milk*
> *⅛ teaspoon grated nutmeg*
> *Dash cayenne*
> *1 teaspoon salt*
> *⅛ teaspoon pepper*
> *¾ cup grated American cheese*
> *4 slices firm white bread, toasted*
> *4 slices cooked white meat of chicken, about ¼" thick*
> *8 slices bacon, fried crisp and drained*
> *¼ cup grated Parmesan cheese*

Heat butter or margarine in a medium-sized saucepan; blend in flour; cook 1 minute. Gradually add cream or milk, stirring as adding. Cook slowly, stirring, until thickened and smooth. Mix in cayenne, salt, pepper, and cheese. Cook slowly until cheese melts. Put each toast slice in a small oven-proof dish or place them all on a cookie sheet. Top each with a slice of chicken and ¼ of the sauce. Top each with 2 slices bacon and 1 tablespoon grated cheese. Put under preheated broiler about 5 minutes, until bubbly and golden. Serves 4.

Cheese-Ham Sandwich A La Suisse

This is a good sandwich for a ladies' luncheon or weekend brunch.

8 slices rye bread
About ¼ cup sharp prepared mustard
8 slices boiled ham
4 eggs, separated
⅛ teaspoon grated nutmeg
Salt, pepper
1 cup grated Parmesan cheese
Paprika

Cut crusts from bread; toast each slice on one side under preheated broiler. Spread each untoasted side with mustard and top with a slice of ham. Combine egg yolks and nutmeg in a small bowl; season with salt and pepper; beat until light and creamy. Beat egg whites with ½ teaspoon salt in a medium-sized bowl until stiff. Fold in egg yolks and cheese. Pile lightly on sandwiches. Sprinkle with paprika. Put under preheated broiler about 5 minutes, until puffy and golden. Serves 4.

Giant Stuffed Hamburger Sandwiches

These hearty open-faced hamburgers are good sandwiches for dinner or a weekend outdoor meal. Cook in the broiler, or grill over hot coals if desired.

2 pounds ground beef
2 cloves garlic, crushed

2 teaspoons salt
¾ teaspoon pepper
¼ cup minced onion
¼ cup chili sauce
2 tablespoons melted butter or margarine
2 tablespoons fresh lemon juice
1 cup soft bread crumbs
2 large sesame, poppy seed or French rolls, split and
   toasted
4 large tomato slices
4 cucumber slices

Combine beef, garlic, 1½ teaspoons salt, and ½ teaspoon pepper in a large bowl. Divide into 8 equal portions. Put on a flat surface and flatten with a spatula into rounds. Combine onion, chili sauce, butter, lemon juice, bread crumbs, ½ teaspoon salt, and ¼ teaspoon pepper in a small bowl. Spoon onto 4 patties and top with remaining patties. Press around edges to completely enclose stuffing. Broil, turning once, about 7 minutes on each side, until cooked to taste. To serve, put on rolls; top with tomato and cucumber slices. Serves 4.

Riviera Tomato-Tuna Sandwich

This is an attractive and nourishing sandwich for a family luncheon or supper.

1 can (6½ or 7 ounces) tuna, drained and flaked
½ cup chopped celery
3 tablespoons grated or minced onion
1 teaspoon anchovy paste
½ cup mayonnaise or salad dressing

½ *teaspoon dried oregano*
1 *teaspoon salt*
¼ *teaspoon pepper*
6 *slices toasted crusty white bread or crusty white roll
  halves*
2 *tablespoons butter or margarine, softened*
4 *teaspoons sharp prepared mustard*
4 *large thick tomato slices*
8 *slices mozzarella cheese*
Paprika

Combine tuna, celery, onion, anchovy paste, mayonnaise or salad dressing, oregano, salt, and pepper in a large bowl. Spread bread or rolls with butter and mustard. Top each with a tomato slice, ¼ of the tuna mixture, and 2 slices of mozzarella cheese. Sprinkle with a little paprika. Put sandwiches on a cookie sheet; bake in preheated 450° oven 10 to 12 minutes, until cheese is melted. Serves 4.

Coney Island Chili Dogs

This well-known frankfurter specialty is a good sandwich for a family supper or children's party.

1 *medium-sized onion, peeled and minced*
1 *tablespoon salad oil*
½ *pound ground beef*
1 *can (6 ounces) tomato paste*
1 *cup water*
2 *tablespoons chili powder*
1 *teaspoon dried oregano*
¾ *teaspoon salt*

⅛ teaspoon pepper
10 frankfurters
10 frankfurter rolls

Sauté onion in heated oil in a medium-sized skillet until tender. Add beef and cook, stirring with a fork, until redness disappears. Spoon off any fat. Stir in tomato paste, water, and seasonings. Cook slowly, uncovered, 10 minutes. Meanwhile, heat or broil frankfurters and heat frankfurter rolls. To serve, put frankfurters in rolls; spoon chili sauce along center of each. Serve at once. Serves 10.

Italian Mozzarella in Carrozza

Mozzarella in carrozza, mozzarella in a carriage, is an appealing fried cheese sandwich that can be prepared in various forms. It originated in Naples and became popular throughout Italy. Serve for brunch or lunch.

½ cup butter or combination of butter and olive oil
4 flat anchovy fillets, drained and minced
1 tablespoon fresh lemon juice
8 slices firm white bread
4 thick slices mozzarella cheese
2 eggs
3 tablespoons milk
Salt, pepper to taste
Olive oil and/or butter or margarine for frying

Heat butter or butter and oil in a small saucepan; add anchovies and lemon juice; keep warm. Remove crusts from bread; top each of 4 slices with a slice of mozzarella. Cover with remaining bread slices. Combine eggs, milk, salt, and pepper in a shallow dish. Dip sandwiches in the mixture to coat well on both sides. Fry sandwiches in heated oil or butter in a large skillet on both sides until cheese is melted and sandwiches are golden. Remove from skillet with a spatula; drain on paper toweling. Serve at once topped with a little of the warm anchovy sauce. Serves 4.

Chicago Club Sandwich

This is an attractive open-faced sandwich for a ladies' luncheon.

4 slices rye bread
4 teaspoons butter or margarine, softened
4 thin slices Swiss cheese
4 lettuce leaves, washed and dried
4 thin slices baked or boiled ham
4 thin slices cooked white meat of turkey or chicken
1 cup bottled or homemade Russian dressing
4 thin tomato slices
4 hard-cooked egg slices
4 sweet pickle slices
8 thin slices bacon, fried crisp and drained

Spread each bread slice with butter or margarine. Place each one on an individual small serving plate. Top each with a slice of cheese, a lettuce leaf, a slice of ham, a slice of turkey or chicken, and ¼ cup Russian dressing. Then top with a tomato slice, an egg slice, a pickle slice, and 2 slices bacon. Serves 4.

Down East Seafood Rolls

In Maine these sandwiches are traditionally made with lobster, but any other seafood may be used. The filled rolls are good for picnics or weekend luncheons.

> *½ cup diced celery*
> *¼ cup minced scallions, with some tops*
> *2 cups diced cooked lobster, scallops, crabmeat or shrimp*
> *½ cup mayonnaise or salad dressing*
> *2 tablespoons chili sauce*
> *2 tablespoons chopped fresh parsley (optional)*
> *Salt, pepper to taste*
> *4 frankfurter rolls, partially split and toasted*

Combine celery, scallions and seafood in a medium-sized bowl. Mix mayonnaise, chili sauce, parsley, salt, and pepper. Add to seafood mixture; mix well. Spoon into warm frankfurter rolls. Serves 4.

New Orleans Poor Boy Sandwich

The Poor Boy sandwich is called Po Boy in New Orleans where it is a cherished local specialty. The name is believed to have derived from the French expression for a tip, *pourboire*, used by children who begged for money and were given sandwiches made with long loaves of crusty French bread. Poor Boys may be made with a wide variety of ingredients such as fried fish fillets, fried oysters or roast meats. This is one appealing version that can be served for a supper or an outdoor meal.

> *2 long loaves crusty French bread, 1 pound each*
> *½ cup olive or salad oil*

2 tablespoons wine vinegar
½ cup minced onion
1 or 2 cloves garlic, crushed
¼ teaspoon dried basil
½ teaspoon salt
⅛ teaspoon pepper
2 cups shredded lettuce
2 large tomatoes, peeled and cubed
½ pound sliced cold cooked lean beef
¼ pound thin slices Cheddar or Swiss cheese
About 3 tablespoons sharp prepared mustard

Split each loaf of bread lengthwise. Combine oil, vinegar, onion, garlic, basil, salt, and pepper. Brush bottom half of each loaf with oil-vinegar mixture. Sprinkle with shredded lettuce. Top with tomato cubes, beef, and cheese slices. Spread top half of each loaf with mustard. Put over bottom halves and press down gently. Cut each loaf into 4 pieces. Serves 4, allowing 2 pieces for each person.

Turkey Shortbread Sandwich

This is an appealing hot sandwich for a company luncheon or supper.

½ cup minced onion
½ cup butter or margarine
1 cup chopped fresh or canned mushrooms
1 tablespoon fresh lemon juice
¼ cup all-purpose flour
2 cups light cream or milk
2 cups diced cooked turkey

2 teaspoons Worcestershire sauce
¾ teaspoon salt
⅛ teaspoon pepper
6 warm baking powder biscuits, halved
6 warm sautéed mushroom caps (optional)
2 tablespoons minced chives

Sauté onion in ¼ cup butter or margarine in a small skillet until tender. Add mushrooms and lemon juice; sauté 4 minutes if fresh, or 2 minutes if canned. Remove from heat and set aside. Heat remaining ¼ cup butter or margarine in a medium-sized saucepan; stir in flour; blend well. Gradually add cream or milk, stirring as adding, and cook slowly, stirring, until thickened and smooth. Add sautéed mushroom mixture, turkey, Worcestershire sauce, salt, and pepper. Cook slowly, covered, about 7 minutes, until flavors are well blended. To serve, spoon turkey mixture between and over each biscuit placed on small plates. Garnish each top with a mushroom cap sprinkled with chives. Serves 6.

Old-Fashioned Baked Bean Sandwich

This is a simple but nourishing sandwich that has long been popular in New England. Serve for a Saturday night supper with coleslaw.

2 cups canned or cooked molasses baked beans, drained
    and chilled
¼ cup minced onion
½ cup chili sauce
Salt, pepper to taste
4 buttered slices brown or rye bread
4 thin slices bacon, fried crisp and crumbled

Combine beans, onion, chili sauce, salt, and pepper in a small saucepan. Heat 10 minutes. Spoon about ½ cup hot bean mixture over each bread slice; top with crisp bacon. Serve with gherkins. Serves 4.

Soups

Hearty soups make great one-dish meals which are fun to prepare and delightful to savor. Superb at brunches or luncheons, they are also excellent for suppers or informal dinners, and can easily star at buffets or late evening parties. A pot or tureen of soup may be the mainstay of a meal whether served out-of-doors, on the porch, in the kitchen, or at the dining room table.

One marvelous advantage of serving a soup is that it is so easy. If prepared beforehand, a soup may be kept in the refrigerator or frozen, and then reheated just prior to the meal. The soup can be ladled directly from either the cooking utensil or an attractive serving dish. The only accompaniments needed with most soups are some kind of bread and a wine or other beverage.

Perhaps the best evidence of the culinary value of soup is its perennial appeal. The saga of soup dates back to the beginnings of cookery when ancient man hit on the idea of filling an animal-skin bag with meat, bones and liquid, along with hot stones to cook the mixture. With the invention of clay containers the ingredients became more varied and were simmered over direct heat. Thus was created the first *pot au feu,* or pot on the fire.

Probably the earliest literary reference to soup is found in the Bible, where one can read in Genesis that Esau sold his birthright to his brother Jacob for "a pottage of lentils." During the many centuries since that time cooks of all nations have utilized the available bounty of land and sea to create an extensive repertoire of national favorites, each distinctively prepared and flavored according to local taste.

During the Dark Ages, a time when man was forced to forage for anything edible to keep alive, soups became the mainstay of the daily diet. Basic creations utilized grains and other accessible foods to provide warmth and nourishment. The first "soup kitchens," which would be revived over and over again in times of need, were established in the monasteries. These enabled countless numbers of hungry and travel-weary unfortunates to survive.

The word for soup evolved, during the Middle Ages, from *sop,* the name for a piece of bread dipped in meat broth. About the twelfth century the broth was called *sop* or *soupe,* and other ingredients were added to the liquid.

We are indebted to soups not only for the establishment of the first restaurant but for the word "restaurant" itself. In 1765 an enterprising Parisian vendor, one Boulanger, began advertising soups on his menu as "magical" *restaurants* (restoratives or pick-me-ups). Not only did his business prosper but his soups became the rage of Paris.

Long acknowledged as a culinary mainstay, soups have been relished at international tables through good times and bad. Settlers in the New World would have perished without them. On their historic voyage the Pilgrims subsisted primarily on soups prepared in large pots suspended from overhead beams in the Mayflower. In the kitchens of the early colonists the predominant cooking utensils were kettles, filled most often with nourishing soups.

When more lavish fare became available and lengthy meals of

many courses were stylish, robust soups were relegated to the unworthy status of common fare. But, thankfully, fashions in gastronomy change, and now the old favorite of our forefathers, enhanced by recipes from around the world, once again holds a place of honor on our menus.

Of infinite variety and flavor, soups have no geographical boundaries. Many are robust and hearty familiar creations while others are subtly seasoned esoteric dishes with strange names. The soup kettle simmering on the stove does not have to be only a pleasant memory from yesteryear. There is no magic or mystique about preparing soups; all that you need is a little time and effort for which you and your guests will be well rewarded.

While soups are age-old favorites, they have particular appeal for the contemporary cook. Utensils, for example, are simple. The primary requirement is a large, heavy pot or kettle made of good material. (The size will vary according to the recipe.) The cover must fit tightly, too. Otherwise, all that is needed is equipment such as sharp knives, cooking spoons, a slotted spoon or skimmer, a long-handled fork, and, depending on the intricacy of preparation, perhaps a few other helpful gadgets. Most kitchens have all the necessary items.

Shopping for the ingredients poses no great problem since most of them are readily available at the nearby grocery. And in times when all of us are concerned about food prices, these one-dish meals can well be considered a boon to the budget. No worthy dish can be put together for a few cents, but in comparison with other choices, excellent soups can be prepared without spending a lot. Most of the fare is simple and honest and is improved by judicious seasoning and slow cooking.

Soup ingredients should be of good quality. This does not necessarily mean that they must be expensive, but it is worthwhile to take time to select fresh food that is in prime condition. There are substitutes available for broths, stocks and bouillons, but those made from scratch will add more flavor to the dish. If wine is used, it too should be of good quality though not a rare vintage.

Hearty soups are made by cooking meat, poultry, seafood, and/or vegetables, and often some form of starch, in a seasoned liquid. They are almost always cooked on top of the stove. The soups do not necessarily have to simmer long. Overcooking may detract from appearance and flavor and result in a loss of valuable nutrients.

Preparation time can vary from several minutes to an hour or more, depending on the recipe. But, with few exceptions, all the work, including the cooking, can be done beforehand. For some soups there are "last minute" additions, such as vegetables and egg yolks or other thickeners. Even so, this entails no great effort.

Most of the following soups can be frozen, but be careful not to overcook them initially since each will undergo additional cooking when it's reheated. In most cases you'll want to shorten the specified cooking time by 5 or 10 minutes. Soups prepared to be frozen should be cooled quickly and thoroughly and then put into appropriate containers, leaving an inch at the top to allow for expansion. Soups may be stored in the freezer for up to 6 months.

Some foods are better added to soups after they have been defrosted and reheated, for example, dumplings, pasta, and vegetables such as potatoes, green peppers, green peas, lima beans, and corn. Season the soup lightly so the seasonings can be checked and corrected when reheating.

Thaw frozen soups at room temperature or by placing the closed containers under running hot water. Reheat over low heat in a covered pot on top of the stove or in a 325° oven. Or slowly reheat without thawing although, of course, this takes longer.

When serving these soups remember that the suggested number of portions in a recipe is a highly negotiable subject, for it will vary according to other items on the menu and the appetite of the diner. Therefore, the number of servings is offered merely as a guideline. The suggestions, however, are on the generous side. It is better to have too much soup than too little. And it can always be reheated and enjoyed at another time.

Soup should be served as attractively as possible. Sometimes it can be offered from the utensil in which it was cooked. But it is particularly delightful when ladled from a colorful tureen.

Thai Shrimp-Chicken Soup

This spicy soup from Thailand is traditionally made with pungent ingredients such as lemon grass, fish sauce, coriander root and leaves, and chili peppers. This is an adaptation. Serve for a luncheon or late evening supper.

> *2 whole chicken breasts, halved*
> *6 cups water*
> *1 small onion, peeled and chopped*
> *1 small bay leaf*
> *2 sprigs parsley*
> *½ teaspoon dried thyme*
> *1 teaspoon salt*
> *⅛ teaspoon pepper*
> *1 clove garlic, crushed*
> *2 teaspoons ground coriander*
> *1½ teaspoons chili powder*
> *1 tablespoon soy sauce*
> *½ pound raw small shelled shrimp, deveined*
> *2 cups sliced mushrooms*
> *6 scallions, with tops, sliced*
> *⅓ cup chopped fresh coriander or parsley*
> *3 cups hot cooked rice*

Remove skin from chicken breasts. Carefully cut meat from bones and pull out pieces of cartilage. Cut meat into strips and set aside. Put bones in a large saucepan. Add water, onion, bay leaf, parsley, thyme, salt, and pepper. Bring to a boil. Lower heat and cook slowly, covered, 1 hour. Strain broth into a saucepan. Combine garlic, coriander, chili powder, and soy sauce. Stir into broth. Bring to a boil. Add chicken, shrimp, and mushrooms. Cook slowly, covered, about 5 minutes, until shrimp turn pink, and chicken is tender. Stir in scallions and fresh coriander or parsley. Remove and discard bay leaf. Serve in bowls over or with rice. Serves 6.

West African Lemony Chicken-Okra Soup

This is a colorful soup that combines chicken, vegetables, and rice. Lemon juice and curry powder enhance the flavor. It is an unusual soup for a company supper.

Juice of 2 lemons
1 broiler-fryer chicken, about 2½ pounds, cut up
6 cups chicken broth or water
1 large onion, peeled and chopped
3 tomatoes, peeled and chopped
1 can (6 ounces) tomato paste
2 cups or 1 can (15½ ounces) sliced okra, drained
⅓ cup uncooked long grain rice
2 teaspoons salt
¼ teaspoon pepper
½ teaspoon ground red pepper
1 teaspoon ground turmeric

Rub lemon juice over chicken pieces. Put in a large kettle with chicken broth or water. Bring to a boil. Lower heat and cook slowly, covered, 12 minutes. Add remaining ingredients and continue to cook slowly about 30 minutes, until chicken and rice are tender. Remove chicken pieces and debone. Cut meat into small pieces and return to kettle. Serves 4 to 6.

Brittany Mixed Fish Soup

This fish soup from France's northwest province of Brittany is named *cotriade* but it is often called Breton bouillabaisse. It does not include shellfish but is made with a large variety of Atlantic fish, using a selection of those from the day's catch, as well as onions, potatoes, and herbs. Use three or more fresh fish that are available in your locale. It is a good dish for a Friday night supper.

> *3 pounds mixed fish (flounder, mackerel, cod, haddock),*
> *cleaned*
> *2 large onions, peeled and sliced thin*
> *1 large clove garlic, crushed*
> *3 tablespoons butter or margarine*
> *6 medium-sized potatoes, peeled and quartered*
> *10 cups water*
> *2 medium bay leaves*
> *1 teaspoon dried thyme*
> *½ teaspoon dried marjoram*
> *4 sprigs parsley*
> *2 teaspoons salt*
> *½ teaspoon pepper*
> *Slices of crusty French bread*

Cut fish into chunks of equal size. Sauté onions and garlic in heated butter or margarine in a large kettle until tender. Add potatoes, water, bay leaves, thyme, marjoram, parsley, salt, and pepper. Bring to a boil. Add prepared fish and lower heat to moderate. Cook, covered, about 25 minutes, until fish and potatoes are tender. Remove and discard bay leaves. Put slices of bread in wide soup plates. Ladle broth over bread. Serve fish and potatoes separately on a platter. Serves 6 to 8.

Hungarian Goulash Soup

Gulyás, the national dish of Hungary, and called goulash in America, is a well-known stew but it is also prepared as a soup. This particular version, made with caraway seeds, marjoram and lemon peel, is not well known. It is especially appropriate for a late evening men's get-together.

4 medium-sized onions, peeled and chopped
2 large cloves garlic, crushed
About ½ cup shortening or salad oil
3 to 4 tablespoons paprika, preferably Hungarian
3 pounds lean beef chuck, cut into 1-inch cubes
2 large tomatoes, peeled and chopped
2 teaspoons caraway seeds
1½ teaspoons dried marjoram
1 teaspoon minced lemon peel
8 cups water
2 teaspoons salt
½ teaspoon pepper
4 medium-sized potatoes, peeled and cubed

Sauté onions and garlic in heated shortening or oil in a large kettle until tender. Stir in paprika; cook 1 minute. Wipe dry beef cubes and brown, several at a time, on all sides. Add tomatoes, caraway seeds, marjoram, lemon peel, water, salt, and pepper. Bring to a boil. Lower heat and cook slowly, covered, 45 minutes. Add potatoes and continue to cook about 20 minutes longer, until potatoes are tender. Serves 10.

Southwestern Meatball Soup

This is a good soup for a late evening meal.

¾ pound ground beef
¾ pound ground pork
⅓ cup uncooked long grain rice
1 egg, slightly beaten
1 teaspoon dried oregano
Salt, pepper
1 medium-sized onion, peeled and minced
1 clove garlic, crushed
2 tablespoons salad oil
½ cup tomato paste
10 cups beef bouillon
½ cup chopped fresh coriander or parsley

Combine beef, pork, rice, egg, oregano, 1 teaspoon salt, and ¼ teaspoon pepper in a large bowl. Shape into small balls, about ¾". Sauté onion and garlic in heated oil in a large kettle until tender. Mix in tomato paste. Add bouillon; season with salt and pepper. Bring to a boil. Add meatballs and reduce heat. Cook slowly, covered, about 30 minutes, until meatballs are cooked. Stir in coriander or parsley. Serves 6 to 8.

German Lentil Soup with Frankfurters

This inexpensive soup is made with dried lentils, a nourishing legume usually brownish in color. Because of their bland flavor lentils should be well seasoned with spices, onions, garlic, and/or vinegar. This is a good soup for a family meal.

2 *medium-sized onions, peeled and chopped*
1 *clove garlic, crushed*
2 *medium-sized carrots, scraped and chopped*
2 *stalks celery, cleaned and chopped*
2 *tablespoons salad oil*
8 *cups water*
2 *cups lentils, washed and drained*
1 *bay leaf*
1½ *teaspoons salt*
¼ *teaspoon pepper*
1 *pound frankfurters, sliced thickly*
2 *tablespoons cider vinegar*

Sauté onions, garlic, carrots, and celery in heated oil in a large kettle for 5 minutes. Add water, lentils, bay leaf, salt, and pepper. Bring to a boil. Lower heat and cook slowly, covered, about 30 minutes, until lentils are just tender. Add frankfurters and cook another 10 minutes. Remove from heat and stir in vinegar. Remove and discard bay leaf. Serves 8.

Maine Fish Chowder

Early settlers in New England created several varieties of a thick soup that they called chowder. The name derived from a large French kettle called *la chaudière,* used by fishermen in the northwestern region of Brittany. A properly prepared chowder is an exceptional treat that should be made with salt pork, fresh fish, and rich milk that is a combination of half milk and half light cream or evaporated milk. Serve with common crackers for a Friday night supper.

¼ *pound salt pork, diced*

4 cups diced raw potatoes
3 medium-sized onions, peeled and sliced
2 teaspoons salt
3 to 3¼ pounds fresh skinned haddock or other white-
fleshed fish with bones in it
2 cups scalded milk
1 tablespoon butter or margarine
Freshly ground pepper to taste

Fry salt pork to render all fat in a heavy kettle and then remove. Add potatoes, onions, and ½ teaspoon salt. Cover with hot water and cook over medium heat, covered, 15 minutes, until potatoes are just tender. Do not overcook. Meanwhile, cut fish into large chunks and put into another saucepan. Add boiling water to cover and 1½ teaspoons salt. Cook slowly, covered, until fish is fork tender, about 15 minutes. Remove from heat. Strain and reserve liquid. Remove any bones from fish. Add fish and strained liquid to potato-onion mixture. Pour in milk and leave on stove long enough to heat through, about 5 minutes. Mix in butter and pepper. Serve at once. Serves 4 to 6.

Danish Pea Soup with Pork

This thick yellow pea soup called *gule aerter* includes bacon or smoked pork and sausages as well as vegetables. Hearty and warming, it is good for a winter supper or luncheon. Serve with dark bread, mustard and beer.

1 pound yellow split peas, washed and drained
2 pounds lean bacon or smoked pork in one piece
3 medium-sized carrots, scraped
1 celery root, washed, peeled and quartered
4 medium-sized leeks, white parts only, cleaned and
washed

2 medium-sized onions, peeled and cut into halves
½ teaspoon dried thyme
1½ teaspoons salt
¼ teaspoon pepper
1 pound pork sausage links, cooked and drained

Soak peas in cold water according to package directions. Put in a large kettle with 6 cups water. Cook slowly, covered, 1½ hours, until tender. Put bacon, carrots, celery root, leeks, onions, thyme, salt, and pepper in another kettle. Cover with water. Cook slowly, covered, 40 minutes, until vegetables and bacon are tender. Take out bacon; slice and keep warm. Remove vegetables and add to cooked split peas with as much of the broth in which the vegetables were cooked as desired to thin the soup. Reheat, if necessary. Ladle soup, including vegetables, into wide soup plates and serve sliced bacon and sausages separately on a platter. Serves 6 to 8.

Petite Marmite

Petite marmite, or small pot, is a rich soup made with beef, chicken and vegetables. The name derives from the earthenware pot, a *marmite,* in which the soup is traditionally cooked and served. It is a specialty in Parisian restaurants and is often served as a clear broth garnished with toasted French bread sprinkled with Parmesan cheese, with the meat and vegetables served separately. The soup requires some time to prepare but it is well worth the effort. An excellent supper dish.

2 medium-sized onions, peeled and sliced
2 tablespoons butter or salad oil
2 pounds beef chuck or other beef in one piece
1 pound beef soup bones
2 pounds chicken wings

3 quarts beef bouillon or water
2 bay leaves
4 whole cloves
4 sprigs parsley
½ teaspoon dried thyme
6 peppercorns, bruised
2½ teaspoons salt
3 medium-sized leeks, white parts only, cleaned and
  sliced thick
4 medium-sized carrots, scraped and cut into 1-inch
  pieces
4 medium-sized white turnips, peeled and quartered
1 loaf French bread, sliced thick and toasted
Grated Parmesan cheese, preferably freshly grated

Sauté onions in heated butter or oil in a large kettle until tender. Add beef, beef bones, chicken wings, bouillon, bay leaves, cloves, parsley, thyme, peppercorns, and salt. Bring slowly to a full simmer. Remove any scum. Cook slowly, covered, for 2½ hours, removing occasionally any scum that has risen to the top. Add leeks, carrots, and turnips. Continue to cook slowly another 30 minutes, until meat and vegetables are tender. Remove kettle from stove. Take out and discard bay leaves, cloves, parsley, and peppercorns. Remove beef, beef bones and chicken wings. Keep broth and vegetables warm over low heat. Cut beef into slices. Remove any meat from beef bones and chicken wings. To serve, put some of beef, chicken and vegetables in individual large soup plates. Cover with hot broth. Serve with toasted French bread and grated cheese. Serves 8 to 10.

Iranian Beef-Yogurt Soup

In Iran rich soups, laced with yogurt and well-flavored with such seasonings as onions and herbs, are called *ashes*. Serve this one for a luncheon.

> ¾ *pound lean ground beef*
> ¼ *cup minced onion*
> 1 *teaspoon salt*
> ⅛ *teaspoon pepper*
> 4 *cups plain yogurt*
> 4 *cups water*
> 2 *tablespoons all-purpose flour*
> 2 *medium-sized eggs, beaten*
> ¼ *cup uncooked long grain rice*
> ⅓ *cup chopped scallions, with some tops*
> ⅓ *cup chopped fresh parsley*
> 2 *teaspoons dried mint (optional)*

Combine beef, onion, salt, and pepper in a medium-sized bowl. Shape into tiny meatballs. Heat yogurt in a large saucepan. Combine ½ cup water, flour, and eggs in a small bowl; mix well. Add with rice to heated yogurt; mix well with a whisk or fork. Stir in remaining water. Cook over a very low fire, stirring constantly, until mixture thickens. Add meatballs and continue to cook slowly, covered, 25 minutes, until rice and meatballs are cooked. Stir in scallions, parsley, and mint; remove from heat. Serve at once. Serves 6 to 8.

South American Shrimp-Spinach Soup

South American and Caribbean cooks prepare a traditional soup called *callaloo* with native ingredients such as seafood, greens, vegetables and seasonings, especially hot peppers. This is a good weekend luncheon soup.

1 large onion, peeled and chopped
2 stalks celery, chopped
3 tablespoons butter or margarine
6 cups water
½ pound smoked ham, diced
2 cups washed spinach leaves
1 cup sliced okra
1 pound shrimp, shelled and deveined
½ teaspoon dried thyme
1½ teaspoons salt
¼ teaspoon pepper
Dash hot sauce

Sauté onion and celery in heated butter or margarine in a large kettle until tender. Add water and ham. Bring to a boil. Cook briskly, covered, 10 minutes. Add remaining ingredients and cook slowly, covered, 12 minutes, until shrimp turn pink. Serves 4.

Viennese Beef Soup

A traditional Austrian soup called *rindsuppe,* beef soup, is made with a variety of vegetables that may differ according to the season. You may also add noodles, rice, or dumplings to the soup. It is a good winter dish for a family meal.

2 to 2½ pounds beef bones, cracked
3 pounds beef chuck
3 quarts water
2½ teaspoons salt
¾ teaspoon pepper
1 large onion, peeled and sliced thin
2 medium-sized leeks, white parts only, cleaned and
*   sliced thin*

2 medium-sized carrots, scraped and sliced thin
1 celery root, pared and cubed
3 small turnips, pared and cubed
2 cups cut up cauliflower
4 sprigs parsley
2 bay leaves
½ teaspoon dried thyme

Scald bones and rinse in cold water. Put beef and water in a large kettle; bring to a boil. Add bones, salt and pepper. Slowly bring to a full simmer; remove any scum from the top. Cook over low heat, partially covered, 1½ hours. Again remove any scum from top. Add remaining ingredients and continue to cook about 40 minutes, until meat and vegetables are tender. Remove and discard parsley and bay leaves. Take out meat and cut into bite-size pieces, discarding any gristle. Return to soup. Serves 8 to 10.

Curried Lamb-Rice Soup

Serve this inexpensive soup made with breast of lamb for a family supper.

2 pounds breast of lamb, cut up
2 tablespoons peanut or salad oil
8 cups water
1½ teaspoons salt
¼ teaspoon pepper
1 large onion, peeled and chopped
2 tablespoons butter or margarine
2 to 3 tablespoons curry powder
⅔ cup uncooked long grain rice
1 can (6 ounces) tomato paste
2 cups fresh or frozen green peas

Wipe lamb dry. Brown in heated oil on all sides in a large kettle. Pour off fat. Add water, salt, and pepper. Bring to a boil. Lower heat and simmer, covered, 1 hour. Remove from heat and take out lamb. Cut meat from bones and return it to kettle, discarding any fat and bones. Sauté onion in heated butter in a small skillet until tender. Mix in curry powder; cook 1 minute. Add, with tomato paste and rice, to soup. Continue cooking another 30 minutes, until rice is cooked. Add peas about 10 minutes before cooking is finished, allowing more time for fresh than frozen peas. Serves 6 to 8.

West Indies Pepper Pot

This highly seasoned West Indian soup, made with meat and a wide variety of vegetables, is colorful and inexpensive. It is an excellent dish for a late supper, preferably served outdoors. Warm cornbread is a good accompaniment.

¼ pound salt pork, diced
1½ pounds short ribs of beef, cut into 3-inch pieces
1½ pounds stew beef, cut into 2-inch cubes
12 cups water
½ teaspoon dried thyme
1½ teaspoons salt
¼ teaspoon pepper
1 large onion, peeled and diced
2 cloves garlic, crushed
2 scallions, with some tops, cleaned and sliced
2 tablespoons salad oil
1 large green pepper, cleaned and chopped
1 package (10 ounces) fresh spinach, washed and trimmed
1 package (10 ounces) fresh kale, washed and trimmed
1 can (15½ ounces) okra, drained

4 medium-sized sweet potatoes, peeled and cubed
1 large tomato, peeled and cubed

Put salt pork and short ribs in a large kettle; brown ribs on all sides. Add stew beef and brown on all sides. Pour in water and slowly bring just to a boil. Skim. Add thyme, salt, and pepper. Lower heat and simmer, covered, 1 hour, occasionally removing any scum that rises to the top. While meat is simmering, sauté onion, garlic, and scallions in heated oil in a skillet until tender. Add green pepper and sauté 1 minute. Remove from heat and set aside. After meat has cooked 1 hour, add sautéed vegetables and other ingredients to the kettle. Continue to cook slowly, covered, about 30 minutes, until vegetables and meat are cooked. Remove from heat and cool slightly. Take out short ribs and cut off and discard any fat. Cube meat and return to kettle. Reheat, if necessary. Serves 8.

Dutch Vegetable Soup with Meatballs

Curry-flavored meatballs in a vegetable soup make an inviting dish for a family dinner.

2 slices stale white bread
⅓ cup milk
1 pound ground veal or beef
1 egg, beaten
2 teaspoons curry powder
¾ teaspoon salt
¼ teaspoon pepper
1 large onion, peeled and minced
1 large carrot, scraped and diced
1 large celery stalk, cleaned and diced
2 tablespoons butter or margarine
1 tablespoon salad oil
6 cups beef bouillon

¼ teaspoon dried thyme or marjoram

Soak bread in milk in a large bowl until soft; mash. Add veal or beef, egg, curry powder, salt, and pepper; mix well. Shape into 1½" balls. Sauté onion, carrot, and celery in heated butter and oil in a large kettle 5 minutes. Add bouillon and thyme or marjoram. Bring to a boil. Lower heat and cook slowly, covered, 20 minutes. Add meatballs and cook about 25 minutes, until vegetables and meatballs are tender. Serves 6.

Soupe Au Pistou

This well known southern French vegetable soup derives its name from the spicy sauce, *pistou*, which is added to the dish. It is a good soup for a weekend meal.

1 large onion, peeled and diced
2 leeks, white parts only, cleaned and chopped
3 tablespoons olive or salad oil
2 large tomatoes, peeled and chopped
12 cups water
2 cups diced potatoes
2 cups cut up green beans
1½ teaspoons salt
¼ teaspoon pepper
2 zucchini, about ¾ pound each, washed, stemmed and diced
1 can (1 pound) cannellini or navy beans, drained
½ cup broken spaghettini or vermicelli
4 cloves garlic, crushed
½ cup chopped sweet basil or 1½ tablespoons dried basil
½ cup grated Parmesan cheese, preferably freshly grated
4 tablespoons olive oil

Sauté onion and leeks in heated oil in a large kettle until tender. Add tomatoes and cook 2 minutes. Pour in water; bring to a boil. Add potatoes, green beans, salt, and pepper. Lower heat and cook slowly, uncovered, 15 minutes. Add zucchini, beans, and spaghettini; cook another 20 minutes, until ingredients are tender. Meanwhile, prepare sauce. Pound garlic and basil in a mortar or bowl with a pestle or spoon to form a paste. Stir in cheese. Add oil, 1 tablespoon at a time, and beat. Just before serving, mix in ½ cup hot soup to thin the paste. Gradually stir into hot soup and serve at once. Pass grated cheese with soup. Serves 12.

Russian Borsch

This hearty version of borsch, beet soup, is from the Ukraine. It differs from other varieties in that it includes garlic, tomatoes, and pork as well as beef and several vegetables. It is one of the best soups from that part of Eastern Europe, and is particularly good when reheated. The soup, served with rye or pumpernickel bread, is good for a winter dinner.

8 medium-sized beets
½ cup cider vinegar
Salt
2 pounds beef chuck
3 cracked soup bones
½ pound lean fresh pork
1 bay leaf
8 peppercorns, bruised
2 sprigs parsley
1 clove garlic, crushed
3 carrots, scraped and sliced
2 medium-sized onions, peeled and chopped

2 medium-sized leeks, white parts only, cleaned and
  sliced
½ small head green cabbage, coarsely chopped
3 medium-sized tomatoes, peeled and chopped
1 to 2 teaspoons sugar
1 cup sour cream at room temperature

Wash beets and cook 7 of them, whole and unpeeled, in ¼ cup vinegar and salted water to cover until tender, about 30 minutes. Drain; peel and cut into julienne strips. Put beef, bones and pork with 10 cups water in a large kettle. Bring to a boil; skim. Add bay leaf, peppercorns, parsley, garlic, carrots, onions, and leeks. Cook slowly, covered, 1½ hours, until meat is tender. Add cooked beets, cabbage and tomatoes. Continue to cook slowly another 30 minutes, until ingredients are tender. Remove from heat. Cut meat into bite-sized pieces, removing any bones and gristle, and discard along with bay leaf, peppercorns, parsley, and garlic. Return cut up meat to kettle. Season with salt, Peel and grate remaining beet. Put into a saucepan with 1 cup hot soup stock, remaining ¼ cup vinegar, and sugar. Bring to a boil. Stir into soup and reheat, if necessary. Ladle soup into soup bowls and garnish with a spoonful of sour cream. Serves 8 to 10.

Note: Four peeled, cubed medium-sized potatoes may be added to soup 20 minutes before it is finished, if desired.

Cuban Black Bean Soup

Black or turtle beans, grown in many varieties, are used extensively in the Caribbean to make soups. One of the best is a spicy thick and dark Cuban specialty that is served with side dishes of rice and cut up raw onions. The soup is good for a weekend brunch.

1 pound dried black beans, washed and drained
8 cups water
2 medium-sized onions, peeled and diced
2 or 3 cloves garlic, crushed
1 medium-sized green pepper, cleaned and diced
½ cup olive or salad oil
2 bay leaves
2 teaspoons salt
½ teaspoon pepper
2 tablespoons wine vinegar
3 cups hot cooked long grain rice
1½ cups chopped onions

Put beans and water in a large kettle. Bring to a boil; boil 2 minutes. Remove from heat and let stand, covered, 1 hour. Meanwhile, sauté onions, garlic, and green pepper in heated oil in a medium-sized skillet until tender. Add, with bay leaves, salt, and pepper, to beans. Bring to a boil. Lower heat and simmer, covered, 2 hours, until tender. Mix in vinegar and cook 5 minutes longer. Remove and discard bay leaves. Serve in soup bowls with side dishes of rice and onions. Serves 8.

Tuscan Minestrone

Minestrone is a well-known thick soup which is prepared in Italy in many variations. The word is derived from the Latin *minestra* "to serve" or "to hand out." Long ago, monks kept large pots of the soup on their monastery stoves to offer hungry travelers. This hearty soup is ideal for a winter buffet or informal supper.

3 slices thin bacon, diced
1 tablespoon olive or salad oil

    1 large onion, peeled and diced
    2 leeks, white parts only, cleaned and chopped
    2 cloves garlic, crushed
    1 large carrot, scraped and diced
    2 cups shredded green cabbage
    2 zucchini, about ½ pound each, washed, stemmed and
      sliced
    1 can (1 pound) tomatoes, undrained and chopped
    1½ cups diced peeled potatoes
    8 cups water
    2 teaspoons salt
    ½ teaspoon pepper
    1 can (1 pound) white or kidney beans, drained
    1 cup small pasta or spaghetti, broken up
    ½ cup grated Parmesan cheese

Combine bacon, oil, onion, leeks, and garlic in a large kettle. Cook over low heat 5 minutes. Add carrot and cabbage; sauté 5 minutes. Add zucchini, tomatoes, potatoes, water, salt, and pepper. Bring to a boil. Lower heat and cook slowly, covered, 25 minutes. Add beans and pasta and cook 15 minutes longer, until pasta is just tender and vegetables are cooked. Serve in large soup bowls sprinkled with cheese. Serves 10 to 12.

Belgian Chicken Waterzooi

A famous Belgian soup from the northern region of Flanders, *Waterzooi* can be made with either chicken or fish. It is a rich lemon-flavored specialty made by simmering the primary ingredients with vegetables, herbs, and spices. The soup is a marvelous dish for a company weekend luncheon.

    2 medium-sized onions, peeled and diced
    2 medium-sized leeks, white parts only, cleaned and thin
      sliced

3 celery stalks, chopped
2 medium-sized carrots, scraped and diced
About 1 cup butter or margarine
4½ to 5 pounds broiler-fryer chickens, cut up, washed
    and dried
6 cups chicken broth or bouillon
1 bay leaf
4 whole cloves
½ teaspoon dried thyme
3 sprigs parsley
6 peppercorns
1½ teaspoons salt
¼ cup all-purpose flour
2 egg yolks
Juice of 1 lemon
1 lemon, sliced
¼ cup chopped fresh parsley

Sauté onions, leeks, celery, and carrots in ¼ cup heated butter or margarine in a large kettle 5 minutes. Remove with a slotted spoon to a plate. Heat ⅓ cup butter in a kettle and sauté chicken pieces, several at a time, on all sides. Add more butter, if needed. Return sautéed vegetables and chicken pieces to kettle. Add chicken broth, bay leaf, cloves, thyme, parsley, peppercorns, and salt. Bring to a boil. Lower heat and cook slowly, covered, about 25 minutes, until chicken is tender. Remove kettle from heat and take out chicken pieces. Put on a platter and keep warm. Strain broth into another pan and keep warm.

Melt 3 tablespoons butter in a saucepan; blend in flour. Gradually add 2 cups hot broth and cook slowly, stirring, until mixture thickens. Stir into remaining broth, stirring as adding. Beat egg yolks slightly with lemon juice. Add a little of hot broth and return to kettle. Mix well; remove from heat at once. Correct seasoning. To serve, pour broth over warm chicken pieces. Garnish with lemon slices and parsley. Serves 8.

Note: The soup can be partially prepared beforehand. But do not add egg yolks and lemon slices until just before serving.

Vegetarian Barley-Vegetable Soup

This is a good soup for an informal lunch or supper.

> *2 medium-sized onions, peeled and diced*
> *2 large carrots, scraped and diced*
> *2 stalks celery, chopped*
> *3 tablespoons butter or margarine*
> *1 can (1 pound, 12 ounces) tomatoes, chopped*
> *8 cups water*
> *1 teaspoon dried basil*
> *½ teaspoon dried thyme*
> *2 teaspoons salt*
> *¼ teaspoon pepper*
> *1 cup pearl barley*
> *2 cups cut up frozen green beans or green peas*
> *1 tablespoon chopped fresh dill*

Sauté onions, carrots, and celery in heated butter or margarine in a large kettle for 5 minutes. Add tomatoes, water, basil, thyme, salt, and pepper. Bring to a boil. Stir in barley and lower heat. Cook slowly, covered, 1½ hours, until barley is tender. Stir in beans or peas during last 10 minutes of cooking. Remove from heat and stir in dill. Serves 10 to 12.

East Indies Mulligatawny

This strongly flavored East Indian chicken soup, popularized and changed considerably by British cooks, can be thin or thick and made with a wide variety of ingredients. The name is derived from a Tamil word meaning "pepper water" and the dish is well seasoned with spices. It is a good soup for a Sunday luncheon.

1 broiler-fryer chicken, about 2½ pounds, cut up
1 medium-sized onion stuck with 4 cloves
2 large carrots, scraped and sliced thick
1 stalk celery, sliced
6 cups chicken broth
1½ teaspoons salt
½ teaspoon pepper
¼ cup butter or margarine
1 large onion, peeled and sliced thin
2 tablespoons turmeric powder
1 teaspoon ground coriander
1 teaspoon cajenne pepper
1 clove garlic, crushed
⅓ cup all-purpose flour
1½ cups grated coconut, preferably unsweetened
2 cups hot cooked long grain rice
1 large lemon, sliced

Put chicken pieces into a large kettle. Add onion with cloves, carrots, celery, chicken broth, salt, and pepper. Bring to a boil. Lower heat and cook slowly, covered, 30 minutes, until chicken is tender. Remove chicken pieces and take off meat from bones. Cut meat into bite-sized pieces. Remove and discard skin and bones. Strain and reserve broth. Sauté onion in heated butter or margarine until tender. Add turmeric, coriander, cayenne, and garlic; cook slowly 1 minute. Stir in flour; blend well. Gradually add strained broth and then the coconut. Cook slowly, stirring, 10 minutes. Add cooked chicken pieces and leave on stove just long enough to heat. Serve in wide bowls. Put cooked rice in a bowl and lemon slices on a plate; pass them to each person to be added to the soup as garnishes. Serves 6.

Provençal Bourride

One of the best French fish dishes from Provence is a thick, creamy soup-stew called *bourride.* Its success depends on one of the region's most popular sauces, *aioli,* a pungent garlic mayonnaise that is stirred into the stock in which the fish was cooked to make a lovely, smooth, yellow sauce. This is an excellent soup for a company weekend luncheon. Serve with boiled potatoes, if desired.

> *3½ pounds mixed firm fleshed white fish (sea bass, rock, haddock, flounder, cod)*
> *6 cups water ˙*
> *½ cup dry white wine*
> *2 tablespoons wine vinegar, preferably white*
> *2 medium-sized onions, peeled and sliced thin*
> *2 bay leaves*
> *1 teaspoon fennel seeds*
> *1 teaspoon dried thyme*
> *2 small strips orange peel, white zest removed*
> *2 teaspoons salt*
> *3 egg yolks*
> *Aioli (recipe below)*
> *1 tablespoon fresh lemon juice (optional)*
> *12 pieces toasted French bread*

When purchasing fish, if you have it filleted, ask that heads, bones, and trimmings be wrapped as well.

Put heads, bones, and trimmings in a large kettle. Add water, wine, vinegar, onions, bay leaves, fennel, thyme, orange peel, and salt. Bring to a boil. Lower heat and cook slowly, partially covered, 30 minutes. Skim off scum occasionally. When cooked, strain broth into a bowl, pressing ingredients with a wooden spoon to extract all juices. Wash kettle and return strained liquid to it. About 15 minutes before serving, bring broth to a boil and add fish, cut in serving pieces. Lower heat and simmer, covered, 5 to 8 minutes, until firm to the touch. Do not overcook. Carefully remove fish with a slotted spoon to a warm platter and cover to keep the fish warm. Then quickly beat egg yolks, one at a time, with a wire whisk into 1 cup of *aioli* sauce in a saucepan. Slowly stir in 1 cup hot fish broth and cook over low heat, stirring constantly until broth is thick enough to coat the whisk lightly. Season with salt and pepper and add lemon juice. To serve, pour broth into a tureen or large bowl and bring to the table with the warm toast, platter of warm fish, and reserved *aioli*. Each person puts two slices of toast in the bottom of an individual, wide soup plate and tops them with one or two pieces of fish and some hot broth. Pass *aioli* separately.

Aioli (Garlic Mayonnaise)

6 medium-sized garlic cloves, peeled and crushed
3 egg yolks at room temperature
¼ to ½ teaspoon salt
White pepper to taste
1½ cups olive oil at room temperature
2 to 3 tablespoons fresh lemon juice

Pound garlic in a mortar or bowl with a pestle or wooden spoon. Add egg yolks, one at a time, and pound together until well blended and thick. Season with salt and pepper. Then begin adding oil, drop by drop, beating constantly with a wire whisk until mixture begins to thicken. Add half remaining oil in a steady stream, beating constantly. Then add lemon juice and remaining oil, still beating steadily, until thickened and smooth. Put 1 cup sauce in a small bowl to be added to the soup and put remaining sauce in another small bowl or saucepan to be passed with soup at the table.

Note: The *Aioli* can be prepared beforehand or may be made while the soup stock is cooking. It can also be prepared in an electric blender if the oil is added very slowly.

Pizzas and Pies

Pizzas and main dish pies have particular appeal for informal meals served at midday or any time during the evening. They are easy to fix, can be prepared beforehand, are inexpensive, and can be handily served without any fuss or bother.

Pizza, the open-faced pastry round topped with various colorful and tasty foods has become a favorite in America and many other countries. It originated, however, as a peasant dish in and around Naples, Italy, where leftover bread dough was flattened into a disc, coated with olive oil, topped with tomatoes and mozzarella cheese, and baked in a very hot oven until tender and softly crisp. The word pizza in Italian means pie.

Later, a few other Italian favorite foods such as garlic, anchovies, capers, and perhaps oregano and basil, were added to the basic dish. But pizza remained essentially a simple pie which was enjoyed as an inexpensive meal or snack in *pizzerias*.

Pizza eventually became known in other Italian cities where cooks created new versions of the dish by adding to it food toppings they preferred. The pie was introduced to America by immigrants from Naples during the nineteenth century. The pizza mania, however, began after World War II when pizzerias spread from port cities all across the country until virtually every town had at least one of these fast-food outlets.

Pizzas made in America are a far cry from the Neapolitan version, which is usually smaller, made with a different kind of dough, and topped with fresh or canned plum tomatoes rather than tomato paste or sauce. All the many pizza ingredients, such as mushrooms, sausages, peppers, onions, olives, ham, meatballs, seafood, Parmesan or Romano cheese, and various herbs, are primarily American additions.

Almost everyone has enjoyed pizzas in Italian restaurants or other eating places, and many cooks have found that homemade pizzas are both easy and fun to make. A good raised dough forms the crust. Good quality fresh or canned tomatoes or sauce, slices of bland mozzarella cheese, a sprinkling of oregano, olive oil, and perhaps grated Parmesan cheese placed over the dough forms a basic pizza. Other ingredients can be added as one wishes. A hot oven is essential for proper baking.

Pizzas are customarily made in 12-inch glass or metal round pans but they can also be baked on cookie sheets.

Pizza crusts and sauces can be prepared beforehand for either spur-of-the-moment or planned meals. Prepared pizzas freeze well.

While pizzas are made with a single dough crust, hearty meal-in-one pies, filled with meat, poultry, seafood, cheese, or vegetables, can also be made with two crusts. While the crust is generally prepared with pastry, some pies have toppings of bread cubes, biscuits, or other forms of bread, or mashed potatoes.

Pies have been made for centuries all over the world. During the Middle Ages English pie dishes were called "coffins" as the shape was long and thin like a loaf pan. From then until the early nineteenth century English pies were often mixtures of savory and sweet ingredients such as lamb, capon, game, dates, prunes, raisins, and spices.

Although the nursery rhyme says, "four-and-twenty-black-birds" were baked in a pie, some trickery was involved. The birds were put under the pastry after baking and just before serving so they could fly out to surprise diners at the table. Because creations of this sort included noisy magpies, the name pie is believed to have derived from the bird's habit of collecting oddments. Certainly the early English pies included an exotic assortment of ingredients.

In Britain savory pies such as veal and ham, pork, mutton, game, beefsteak and kidney, known as pasties or pies, are still enjoyed for meals, snacks, and outdoor outings.

Colonial Americans inherited their love of pies from the English, although later, other European favorites such as the French quiche and flan became popular fare.

Until the Revolution deep pastry pies were cooked with a top, but thrifty housewives realized that flat pies with only a bottom crust needed less filling.

Today we have a superb heritage, both from European and American cooks, of easy to make and innovative pies that are versatile and substantial main dishes. They can be served hot, barely warm, or at room temperature, and are perfect for picnics as well as home meals.

The following collection of pizzas and pies includes selections suitable for any occasion.

Basic Pizza Crust

This basic yeast dough, rolled to fit a 12-inch pizza pan, makes two crusts. They can be topped with a diverse selection of ingredients and then baked until the crusts are golden brown.

1 package active dry yeast
Pinch sugar
1⅓ cups very warm water
4 cups all-purpose flour
1½ teaspoons salt
2 tablespoons salad oil

Sprinkle yeast and a pinch of sugar over ⅓ cup warm water (120°) in a small bowl. Let stand 2 or 3 minutes; stir until yeast is dissolved. Sift flour and salt into a large bowl. Make a well in center and pour in yeast mixture, 1 cup warm water and the oil. Mix to form a ball and turn out on a floured surface. Knead about 10 minutes, until dough is smooth and elastic. Put in a greased large bowl and let rise, covered with a light towel, in a warm place until doubled in bulk, about 2 hours. Punch dough down and divide into two halves. Knead each half 1 or 2 minutes. Flatten with palms of hands and stretch dough by pulling to form a circle. Roll with a rolling pin on both sides to develop a circle with a diameter of 14 to 15 inches. During kneading and rolling add a little more flour to dough if it is at all sticky. Put each circle of dough on an oiled 12-inch pizza pan and push evenly with fingers until it is stretched to fit the pan. Crimp edges to form a rim. Let rest 10 minutes. Top with desired pizza ingredients and bake in a preheated 425° oven about 25 minutes, until the crust is golden and the filling is bubbly hot. Makes 2 pizza crusts.

Pizza Sauce

This herb-flavored tomato sauce can be easily prepared and refrigerated or frozen to be used as needed. It may be puréed, if desired.

> 1 cup minced onions
> 2 garlic cloves, crushed
> 3 tablespoons olive or salad oil
> 1 can (1 pound, 12 ounces) crushed tomatoes or Italian
>   plum tomatoes, chopped
> 1 can (6 ounces) tomato paste
> 1 tablespoon sugar
> 2 teaspoons dried oregano
> 1 teaspoon dried basil
> 1 bay leaf
> 1½ teaspoons salt
> ¼ teaspoon pepper

Sauté onions and garlic in heated oil in a medium-sized skillet until tender. Stir in remaining ingredients; mix well. Bring sauce to a boil. Reduce heat and simmer, uncovered, 1 hour, stirring occasionally. Remove and discard bay leaf. For a smoother sauce, purée. Makes 4 cups.

Bruce Stout's Party Pizza

Bruce Stout, a graduate of Rutgers University, created this super pizza variation. The dough, stretched rather than rolled, becomes light and crisp, and the tomato sauce is interestingly flavored with honey and cinnamon. The seasonings may be added according to taste. It is a great pizza for an informal get-together.

> 1 package active dry yeast
> 1 cup very warm water
> 1 teaspoon sugar
> About 3¾ cups all-purpose flour

4 tablespoons salad oil
1 teaspoon salt
Pizza Sauce (recipe below)
24 ounces part skim mozzarella cheese, shredded

Combine yeast, water, and sugar in a large bowl. Let stand 5 minutes; stir until dissolved. Add 2 cups flour, 2 tablespoons oil, and salt; mix well. Add 1 cup flour and mix to form a semi-dry ball. Put remaining ¾ cup flour on a wooden board and knead flour into dough ball. Knead about 10 minutes, until dough is smooth and elastic. Add a little more flour, if needed. Form into a ball and put in large bowl with 2 tablespoons oil. Roll until completely covered with oil. Let rise, covered with a light towel, in a warm place until doubled in bulk, about 2 hours, Punch down dough and divide into two halves. With fingers, spread each half to fit two lightly greased 12-inch pizza pans. Cover each with half the sauce. Sprinkle each with half the mozzarella cheese. Bake in a preheated 425° oven about 25 minutes, until crust is golden and filling is bubbly hot. Traditional toppings such as sliced mushrooms, onions, green peppers, and additional cheese may be used to garnish the pizza, if desired. Cut into pie-shaped wedges. Makes 2 pizzas. Each pizza serves 4 to 6.

Pizza Sauce

1 can or jar (15½-16 ounces) spaghetti sauce
¼ cup honey
1 teaspoon dried basil
½ teaspoon dried oregano
1 teaspoon garlic salt
1 teaspoon salt
¼ teaspoon pepper
1 1-inch piece cinnamon

1 medium-sized onion, peeled and chopped
1 large green pepper, cleaned and chopped
2 cans (4 ounces each) sliced mushrooms, drained
1 can (6 ounces) tomato paste

Combine first 8 ingredients in a medium-sized saucepan. Simmer, uncovered, 30 minutes. Add onion, pepper, and mushrooms and continue to simmer 30 minutes longer. Remove from heat. Remove and discard cinnamon piece. Add tomato paste while sauce is still hot; mix well.

Neapolitan Pizza

This is a classic tomato, cheese, and herb pizza from Naples which can be made with coarsely chopped fresh tomatoes or a thick tomato sauce.

1 (12-inch) pizza crust, unbaked
2 cups coarsely chopped tomatoes or pizza sauce
½ pound mozzarella cheese, shredded
12 flat anchovy fillets, drained
½ teaspoon dried oregano
½ teaspoon dried basil
Pepper to taste
1½ tablespoons olive oil

Arrange pizza crust in 12-inch pan. Spread with chopped tomatoes or pizza sauce. Sprinkle with cheese. Top with anchovy fillets, oregano, basil, and pepper. Sprinkle with oil. Bake in a preheated 425° oven about 25 minutes, until crust is golden and filling is bubbly hot. Cut into pie-shaped wedges. Serves 4 to 6.

Niçoise Tuna Pizza

An inexpensive pizza to prepare on the spur of the moment with basic ingredients. It is excellent for a family supper.

1 large onion, peeled
3 tablespoons olive or salad oil
1 can (8 ounces) tomato sauce
1 can (6 ounces) tomato paste
1 teaspoon dried oregano
1 teaspoon sugar
½ teaspoon salt
Dash pepper
1 (12-inch) pizza crust, unbaked
2 cans (7 ounces each) tuna, drained and flaked
½ cup sliced olives
½ pound mozzarella cheese, shredded

Cut onion in half from top to bottom; slice thinly. Sauté in heated oil in a medium-sized skillet until tender. Add tomato sauce and paste, oregano, sugar, salt, and pepper. Cook slowly, uncovered, 10 minutes. Arrange pizza crust in a 12-inch pan. Spread with sauce and tuna. Top with olives and cheese. Bake in a preheated 425° oven about 25 minutes, until crust is golden and filling is bubbly hot. Cut into pie-shaped wedges. Serves 4.

Mediterranean Meatball-Zucchini Pizza

This hearty pizza is an excellent entrée for a company luncheon or supper. It is attractively decorated with colorful zucchini slices. A good choice for a meal after a sporting event.

1 pound ground beef
½ cup Italian seasoned bread crumbs

¼ cup tomato juice
1 egg
1 tablespoon instant minced onion
1½ teaspoons salt
¼ teaspoon pepper
5 tablespoons salad oil
1½ cups tomato sauce
1 medium-sized zucchini, washed, stemmed and sliced
*   thin*
1 (12-inch) pizza crust, unbaked
1 cup pizza sauce
⅓ cup grated Parmesan cheese

Combine beef, bread crumbs, tomato juice, egg, onion, salt, and pepper in a large bowl. Shape into small balls, about 1 inch. Brown several at a time on all sides in 3 tablespoons heated oil in a large skillet. Add tomato sauce and cook slowly, covered, 25 minutes. Sauté zucchini slices in 2 tablespoons heated oil in a medium-sized skillet until just tender. Arrange pizza crust in a 12-inch pan. Spread with pizza sauce. Top with meatballs and sauce, spreading evenly. Arrange zucchini slices around edge of crust and to form a circle in the center. Sprinkle with cheese. Bake in a preheated 425° oven about 25 minutes, until crust is golden and filling is bubbly hot. Serves 4 to 6.

Pizza Siciliana

This pizza from Sicily has a well-seasoned topping starring pepperoni, anchovies, capers, and black olives.

1 large onion, peeled and sliced
2 garlic cloves, crushed
2 tablespoons olive or salad oil

2 cups coarsely chopped tomatoes
1 (12-inch) pizza crust, unbaked
½ pound pepperoni, sliced thin
½ pound mozzarella cheese, slivered
12 flat anchovies, drained
2 tablespoons drained capers
12 pitted black olives
¼ cup grated Parmesan cheese
½ teaspoon dried oregano

Sauté onion and garlic in heated oil in a small skillet. Add tomatoes and cook 1 minute. Arrange pizza crust in a 12-inch pan. Spread with tomato-onion mixture. Top with remaining ingredients. Bake in a preheated 425° oven about 25 minutes, until crust is golden and filling is bubbly hot. Cut into pie-shaped wedges. Serves 4 to 6.

Riviera Ratatouille Pizza

This savory pizza is topped with the well-known French vegetable combination called ratatouille. It is a good choice for an outdoor meal or picnic.

1 medium-sized eggplant, washed and stemmed
Salt
1 large onion, peeled and chopped
2 cloves garlic, crushed
About ¾ cup olive oil or mixture of olive and salad oils
2 small zucchini, washed, stemmed, and sliced thin
1 medium-sized green pepper, cleaned and chopped
2 large tomatoes, peeled and chopped
1 teaspoon dried basil
½ teaspoon dried oregano

¼ *teaspoon pepper*
1 *(12-inch) pizza crust, unbaked*
1 *cup pizza sauce*
¼ *pound mozzarella cheese, shredded*

Cut eggplant into small cubes. Put in a colander and sprinkle with salt. Let drain 30 minutes. Pat dry with paper toweling. Sauté onion and garlic in 2 tablespoons heated oil in a large skillet until tender. Add eggplant cubes and sauté, several at a time, until soft, adding more oil as needed. Remove to a plate. Add zucchini and sauté until soft. Return eggplant to skillet. Add green pepper, tomatoes, basil, oregano, 1 teaspoon salt, and pepper. Cook slowly, covered, 45 minutes, until vegetables are tender. Arrange pizza crust in a 12-inch pizza pan. Spread with pizza sauce. Top with eggplant mixture, using all of it or 3 cups. Sprinkle with cheese. Bake in a preheated 425° oven about 35 minutes, until crust is golden and filling is bubbly hot. Cut into pie-shaped wedges. Serves 4 to 6.

Southern Eggplant Pizza

This modern southern specialty is made with an eggplant "crust" and tomato topping. A good brunch or luncheon main dish.

1 *medium-sized eggplant, washed and stemmed*
Salt
2 *eggs, beaten*
About ¾ cup all-purpose flour
Pepper
About ½ cup olive or salad oil or mixture of both
1½ *cups pizza sauce*
⅓ *cup grated Parmesan cheese*

Cut eggplant crosswise into very thin slices. Cut large slices into halves. You will want about 50 slices. Put slices into a colander and sprinkle with salt. Let drain 30 minutes. Pat dry with paper toweling. Dip slices in beaten egg and then in flour seasoned with salt and pepper. Fry several at a time on both sides in heated oil in a large skillet until tender and golden, adding more oil as needed. Drain on paper toweling. Arrange slices in circles overlapping each other to cover the bottom and sides of a 12-inch pizza pan. Sprinkle with sauce and cheese. Bake in a preheated 400° oven 10 minutes. Cut into pie-shaped wedges. Serves 4.

Sausage-Vegetable Pizza

Green peppers, mushrooms, and Italian sausage add color and zest to this pizza that requires little preparation.

>   *1 medium-sized green pepper, cleaned and cut into*
>   *slivers*
>   *1 small onion, peeled and sliced*
>   *1 can (4 ounces) mushroom slices, drained*
>   *2 tablespoons olive or salad oil*
>   *1 (12-inch) pizza crust, unbaked*
>   *2 cups tomato or pizza sauce*
>   *½ pound mozzarella cheese, shredded*
>   *½ pound Italian sausage, sliced thin*

Sauté green pepper, onion, and mushrooms in heated oil in a small skillet 3 minutes. Remove from heat. Arrange pizza crust in a 12-inch pan. Spread with tomato or pizza sauce. Top with cheese, sausages, and sautéed vegetables. Bake in a preheated 425° oven 25 minutes, until crust is golden and filling is bubbly hot. Cut into pie-shaped wedges. Serves 4 to 6.

Provençal Onion-Olive Pizza

This French version of pizza, called *pissaladière,* is a specialty of Nice, a lovely port city, but it is enjoyed throughout Provence. It is a good luncheon or picnic specialty.

*8 medium-sized onions (about 6 cups), peeled and sliced
    thin
2 cloves garlic, crushed
½ cup olive or salad oil
2 tablespoons butter or margarine
1 teaspoon salt
¼ teaspoon freshly ground pepper
1 (12-inch) pizza crust, unbaked
1 can (2 ounces) flat anchovies, drained
12 pitted large black olives*

Sauté onions and garlic in heated oil and butter in a medium-sized skillet until tender, being careful not to brown. Remove from heat; add salt and pepper. Cool. Arrange pizza crust in a 12-inch pan. Spread with onion mixture. Make a lattice pattern with anchovies over onions. Place an olive in center of each square. Brush lightly with oil. Bake in a preheated 425° oven about 25 minutes, until crust is golden and filling is bubbly hot. Cool slightly. Cut into pie-shaped wedges. Serves 4 to 6.

California Zucchini Pie

This colorful pie features zucchini, the attractive green and yellow striped variety of summer squash developed in Italy, which is also known as Italian squash or vegetable marrow. The pie is a delectable dish for a weekend brunch.

*2 medium-sized zucchini, about ½ pound each, washed
    and stemmed*
1 medium-sized onion, peeled
About 3 tablespoons olive or salad oil
½ teaspoon dried oregano
1½ teaspoons salt
¼ teaspoon pepper
4 eggs
½ cup sour cream at room temperature
½ cup grated Parmesan cheese
1 (9-inch) pie shell, baked 10 minutes and cooled

Wipe zucchini dry and slice thin. Cut onion in half from top to bottom; slice thin. Sauté onion in heated oil in a medium-sized skillet until tender. Push aside and sauté zucchini slices, several at a time, until tender, adding more oil if needed. Remove to a bowl when cooked. Add oregano, salt, and pepper; mix well. In another bowl combine eggs, sour cream, and cheese. Add to zucchini. Turn into a pie shell, spreading evenly. Bake in a preheated 375° oven about 30 minutes, until puffed and golden and blade of a knife inserted into filling comes out clean. Serves 4.

English Cottage Pie

This old English dish, made of lamb, gravy, and seasonings, with a topping of mashed potatoes, is now subject to many variations. This version also includes bacon. Serve the pie for a family supper.

3 slices thin bacon, chopped
1 large onion, peeled and sliced

2 cups brown gravy
1 tablespoon Worcestershire sauce
½ teaspoon dried marjoram
1½ teaspoons salt
¼ teaspoon pepper
3 cups diced cooked lamb
2 cups seasoned mashed potatoes
2 tablespoons butter or margarine
½ teaspoon paprika

Fry bacon in a small skillet until crisp. Remove, drain, and set aside. Spoon off all fat but 1 tablespoon. Add onion and sauté until tender. Add gravy, Worcestershire sauce, marjoram, salt, and pepper. Cook slowly 2 minutes to blend flavors. Spoon lamb into a 2½ quart casserole. Cover with fried bacon and sauce. Spread with potatoes and dot with butter. Garnish top with paprika. Bake in preheated 425° oven 20 minutes, until bubbly hot. Serves 6.

Summer Salmon Pie

An attractive main dish for a ladies' luncheon.

1 envelope unflavored gelatine
1¼ cups tomato juice
½ cup minced celery
½ cup minced green pepper
2 cans (about 7 ounces each) salmon, cleaned, drained
    and flaked
½ cup sour cream
2 tablespoons grated onion
2 tablespoons fresh lemon juice

¼ cup chopped fresh parsley
Salt, pepper to taste
1 (9-inch) pie shell, baked

Sprinkle gelatine over tomato juice in a small saucepan. Heat about 2 minutes, stirring to dissolve gelatine. Chill until slightly thickened. Combine with remaining ingredients, except pastry shell, in a large bowl. Turn into pastry shell. Chill until set. Serves 6.

Shepherd's Pie

This meat-vegetable pie is an American adaptation of the English cottage pie which was once called shepherd's pie. In earlier times shepherds took the dish with them to heat over an open fire as they tended their flocks. A good dish to make for supper with leftover roast beef.

2 cups cut up cooked beef
2 cups brown gravy
1 cup sliced cooked carrots
1 cup cooked green peas
1 can (1 pound) small white onions, drained
2 cups seasoned mashed potatoes
1 egg yolk, beaten

Combine beef, gravy, carrots, peas, and onions in a medium-sized saucepan. Heat 2 minutes to blend flavors. Spoon into a 2½ quart casserole. Combine potatoes and egg yolks and arrange in a ring around edge of casserole. Bake in a preheated 400° oven 20 minutes. Serves 4.

Welsh Leek-Cheese Pie

This pie is from Wales where the leek is not only a favorite food but also the national emblem. In ancient times a Welsh king, about to lead his men into battle against a neighboring foe, ordered his soldiers to wear leeks on their helmets so they could be distinguished from their enemies. Because they won the struggle, the leek was chosen as the Welsh symbol. Serve this pie as a luncheon or supper entree.

> *3 large leeks*
> *3 tablespoons butter or margarine*
> *4 slices thin bacon, chopped and fried*
> *1 (9-inch) pie shell, baked 10 minutes and cooled*
> *4 eggs*
> *2 cups light cream or milk*
> *⅛ teaspoon grated nutmeg*
> *1 teaspoon salt*
> *¼ teaspoon pepper*
> *⅓ cup grated Parmesan cheese*

Wash leeks well to remove all dirt; trim roots; chop finely the white parts. Sauté in heated butter or margarine in a medium-sized skillet until tender. Put with bacon into pie shell, spreading evenly. Combine eggs, cream or milk, nutmeg, salt, and pepper in a bowl. Stir in cheese; mix well. Pour over leeks and bacon. Bake in preheated 375° oven about 35 minutes, or until blade of a knife inserted into filling comes out clean. Remove from oven and cool slightly before cutting. Serves 4 to 6.

Italian Beef-Spaghettini Pie

An inexpensive and nutritious dish to serve for a family meal. It can be prepared ahead of time and frozen, if desired.

⅓ cup minced onions
5 tablespoons butter or margarine
1 pound ground beef
¼ cup tomato paste
1 cup dry red wine
⅛ teaspoon grated nutmeg
1 teaspoon salt
⅛ teaspoon pepper
1 cup sliced mushrooms, canned or fresh
⅓ cup chopped fresh parsley
8 ounces spaghettini, cooked and drained
½ cup grated Parmesan cheese
½ cup fine dry bread crumbs

Sauté onions in 1 tablespoon heated butter or margarine in a medium-sized skillet until tender. Add beef and cook over medium heat, mincing with a fork, until redness disappears. Add tomato paste, wine, nutmeg, salt, and pepper. Cook slowly, uncovered, 15 minutes. Remove from heat and add mushrooms and parsley. Spoon into a 10-inch pie plate. Combine hot spaghettini with remaining 4 tablespoons butter and ¼ cup cheese. Toss with two forks to mix well. Spoon over meat-mushroom mixture, spreading evenly. Sprinkle with bread crumbs and ¼ cup cheese. Bake in a preheated 400° oven about 20 minutes, until hot and bubbly and golden on top. Serves 4.

Greek Spinach Pie

This attractive flaky pie called *spanakopitta,* made with paper-thin sheets of pastry sold as phyllo or filo in specialty food stores, is excellent for a women's luncheon. The spinach filling is flavored with cheese and dill.

1 package (10 ounces) frozen chopped spinach, defrosted

½ cup chopped scallions, with some tops
1 tablespoon salad oil or butter
2 cups small-curd cottage cheese
1 cup crumbled Feta cheese or grated Muenster cheese
¼ cup chopped fresh parsley
2 tablespoons chopped fresh dill
1½ teaspoon salt
¼ teaspoon pepper
½ pound phyllo sheets
About ¾ cup melted butter or margarine

Pour off any liquid from spinach. Put into a large bowl. Sauté scallions in heated oil or butter until tender. Add to spinach. Then add cheeses, parsley, dill, salt, and pepper; mix well. Grease a 12x9x2-inch baking dish with butter. Place ⅓ of pastry sheets in dish, having first brushed each one quickly with melted butter and folded it over in half. It is necessary to work quickly so phyllo sheets do not dry and become brittle. Spread half spinach mixture over pastry sheets in dish. Repeat with another ⅓ of sheets, brushing each sheet with melted butter. Brush top generously with butter. Bake in preheated 350° oven about 40 minutes, until golden and crisp on top. Cut into squares and serve warm. Serves 6 to 8.

Tuna-Vegetable Pie

This pie can be easily prepared with inexpensive basic ingredients and a bread cube topping. Serve for a Sunday night supper.

1 medium-sized onion, peeled and chopped
½ cup chopped green pepper
3 tablespoons salad oil

1 can (1 pound) tomatoes, chopped
1 teaspoon dried basil
1 teaspoon salt
⅛ teaspoon pepper
2 cans (7 ounces each) tuna, drained and flaked
1 package (10 ounces) frozen French-cut green beans, defrosted
2 cups seasoned bread cubes

Sauté onion and green pepper in heated oil in a large skillet until tender. Add tomatoes, basil, salt, and pepper. Cook slowly, uncovered, 10 minutes, stirring occasionally. Add tuna and green beans; mix well. Turn into a 10-inch pie plate; spread evenly. Top with bread cubes. Bake in preheated 350° oven for 25 minutes. Let stand 10 minutes before serving. Serves 6.

Old-Fashioned Chicken Pot Pie

This old-time American dish is a good choice for a family dinner.

½ cup chopped onion
⅓ cup butter or margarine
¼ cup all-purpose flour
2 cups chicken broth
¼ teaspoon celery salt
1 teaspoon salt
⅛ teaspoon pepper
1 cup cooked green peas
1 cup cooked diced carrots
3 cups cubed cooked chicken
3 cups seasoned mashed cooked potatoes

Sauté onion in heated butter or margarine in a medium-sized saucepan until tender. Add flour; blend well. Gradually add chicken broth; stir over low heat until thick and smooth. Add celery salt, salt, and pepper. Remove from heat. Arrange peas, carrots, and chicken in layers in a 2½-quart casserole. Cover with sauce. Top with mashed potatoes. Bake in preheated 425° oven 20 minutes, until bubbly hot. Serves 6.

French Mushroom Flan

This is an attractive and delicious entrée for a Sunday brunch or luncheon.

> ½ cup diced onions
> ¼ cup butter or margarine
> ¾ pound fresh mushrooms, cleaned and sliced
> 2 teaspoons fresh lemon juice
> ¾ teaspoon salt
> 1 tablespoon all-purpose flour
> Pastry for 1-crust 9-inch pie, baked 10 minutes and
>   cooled
> 3 eggs
> 1½ cups light cream
> ¼ teaspoon pepper
> Generous dash nutmeg
> ½ cup grated Swiss cheese

Sauté onions in heated butter or margarine in a medium-sized skillet until tender. Add mushrooms, lemon juice, and ½ teaspoon salt; sauté 3 minutes. Stir in flour; cook 1 minute. Remove from heat and cool. Turn into pastry shell, spreading evenly. Beat eggs in a bowl. Add cream, ¼ teaspoon salt, pepper, and nutmeg; beat to mix well. Pour over mushrooms. Sprinkle with cheese. Bake in preheated 375° oven 45 minutes, until puffed and golden and custard is set. Cool slightly before cutting into wedges. Serves 4 to 6.

Swedish Fish-Mushroom Pie

A good dish for a family dinner.

> *4 scallions, with some tops, cleaned and sliced*
> *3 tablespoons butter or margarine*
> *1 can (4 ounces) sliced mushrooms, drained*
> *2 teaspoons fresh lemon juice*
> *2 cups flaked cooked white-fleshed fish (cod, flounder, halibut or tuna)*
> *¼ cup chopped fresh parsley*
> *Pastry for 1-crust deep 9-inch pie, baked 10 minutes and cooled*
> *1¼ cups milk, scalded*
> *3 eggs, beaten*
> *1 teaspoon salt*
> *¼ teaspoon pepper*
> *4 slices crisp fried bacon, drained and crumbled*

Sauté scallions in heated butter or margarine in a small skillet 1 minute. Add mushrooms and lemon juice; sauté 1 minute. Combine with fish and parsley. Turn into pastry shell, spreading evenly. Combine milk, eggs, salt, and pepper. Pour over fish mixture. Top with bacon. Bake in preheated 425° oven 20 minutes. Reduce heat to 325° and continue cooking about 12 minutes longer, until puffed and golden and custard is set. Serves 4.

Maine Lumberjack Pie

In northern Maine a meat-filled pie of French-Canadian origin became staple fare for lumberjacks working in the woods during the long cold winters. The pies could be made in large batches, frozen, stored in a cold place, and then simply reheated in an oven. They also became traditional fare for Christmas and New Year's Eve suppers. Serve for supper or a late evening meal.

2 pounds diced pork shoulder
1 medium-sized onion, peeled and diced
½ teaspoon dried sage or thyme
¼ teaspoon ground mace or nutmeg
¼ teaspoon ground cinnamon
1½ teaspoons salt
¼ teaspoon pepper
½ cup water
2 cups mashed potatoes
Standard pastry for 2-crust 9-inch pie, unbaked

Combine pork, onion, sage or thyme, mace or nutmeg, cinnamon, salt, pepper, and water in a medium-sized saucepan. Bring to a boil. Lower heat and cook slowly, covered, 45 minutes. Remove pork to a bowl; reserve liquid. Add potatoes and ½ cup reserved liquid to pork. Cool. Roll out slightly more than half the pastry and line a 9-inch pie pan with it. Spoon pork-potato mixture over pastry, spreading evenly. Cover with remaining pastry. Trim edges and flute, pressing with a fork or fingers. Cut several slits in top. Bake in a preheated 450° oven 15 minutes. Reduce heat to 350° and bake 35 minutes longer, until crust is golden and flaky. Serves 4 to 6.

Quiche Lorraine

The classic *quiche Lorraine,* a specialty of France's Alsace-Lorraine region, is made with bacon, cream, and eggs, without cheese. Modern versions of the open-faced tart or pie, however, generally include grated cheese. The savory mixture can be cooked in a flaky crust in a metal *flan* ring placed on a cookie sheet, in a quiche dish, or in a regular 9- or 10-inch pie pan. Given below are two recipes for two traditional French quiches. Serve for a brunch or luncheon.

> *8 slices crisp fried bacon, drained and crumbled*
> *Pastry for 1-crust 9-inch pie, baked 10 minutes and*
>   *cooled*
> *4 eggs*
> *2 cups heavy cream*
> *½ teaspoon salt*
> *¼ teaspoon pepper*
> *Dash grated nutmeg*
> *2 tablespoons butter or margarine*

Sprinkle bacon over bottom of pastry shell. Beat eggs in a large bowl. Add cream, salt, pepper, and nutmeg; mix well. Pour over bacon. Cut butter into tiny pieces and distribute over top. Bake in preheated 375° oven 45 minutes, until puffed and golden and custard is set. Cool slightly before cutting into wedges. Serves 4 to 6.

Cheese Quiche

Combine 2 cups (½ pound) grated Swiss cheese and 1 tablespoon all-purpose flour in a bowl. Sprinkle evenly over bottom of pastry shell described in above recipe. Cover with 2 cups light cream, 1 teaspoon salt, ¼ teaspoon pepper, and the 2 tablespoons diced butter. Bake as in above recipe. Serves 4 to 6.

Hamburger-Vegetable Pie

This pie features a flavorful ground beef "crust" and colorful zucchini-tomato filling. Serve for an informal company dinner.

1 pound ground beef
½ cup Italian flavored bread crumbs
¼ cup tomato sauce
1 egg
1½ teaspoons salt
¼ teaspoon pepper
1 large onion, peeled
3 tablespoons salad oil
2 medium-sized zucchini, washed, stemmed and sliced
1 cup tomato sauce
½ teaspoon dried oregano
6 thin strips mozzarella cheese

Combine beef, bread crumbs, tomato sauce, egg, salt, and pepper in a large bowl. Turn into a 10-inch pie plate and shape over bottom and sides to form a "crust." Cut onion in half from top to bottom; slice. Sauté in heated oil in a large skillet until just tender. Wipe dry zucchini slices and sauté several at a time until just tender. Add tomato sauce and oregano and cook slowly, covered, 10 minutes. Remove from heat. Bake beef "crust" in a preheated 450° oven 10 minutes. Drain off any fat. Reduce heat to 350°. Spoon zucchini filling into "crust" and top with mozzarella strips. Bake pie another 20 minutes. Cut into pie-shaped wedges. Serves 6.

Chesapeake Bay Oyster-Potato Pie

This is an excellent entrée for a small luncheon or late evening supper starring a delectable specialty, oysters.

Standard pastry for 2-crust 9-inch pie, unbaked
2 cups thinly sliced potatoes, slightly undercooked
1 pint shucked oysters, with liquor
4 hard cooked eggs, shelled and sliced
¼ cup butter or margarine
¼ teaspoon celery salt
1 tablespoon fresh lemon juice
¼ teaspoon pepper

Roll out slightly more than half the pastry and line a 9-inch pie pan with it. Put potato slices over it. Remove oysters from container, reserving liquor, and spoon over potatoes. Top with egg slices. Dot with butter. Sprinkle with celery salt, lemon juice, and pepper. Cover with remaining pastry. Trim and flute edges, pressing with a fork or fingers. Cut several slits in top. Bake in preheated 400° oven 10 minutes. Lower heat to 375° and bake 30 minutes, until crust is golden and flaky. Let stand a few minutes before serving. Serve with oyster sauce (recipe below). Serves 6.

Oyster Sauce

2 tablespoons butter or margarine
2 tablespoons all-purpose flour
1 cup light cream or milk
Oyster liquor plus water to equal ½ cup
Salt, pepper to taste

Melt butter or margarine in a medium-sized saucepan. Mix in flour. Gradually add cream or milk and then oyster liquor, stirring as adding. Cook slowly, stirring, until thickened and smooth. Season with salt and pepper. Serve hot with pie.

English Steak and Kidney Pie

This well-known steak and kidney stew, covered with pastry and baked, may be served hot or lukewarm. It is a specialty of English pubs. Serve for a weekend breakfast or brunch.

1 beef kidney
Salt
1½ pounds round steak, cut into 1-inch pieces
⅓ cup all-purpose flour
1 small onion, peeled and minced
¼ cup butter or margarine
3 cups beef bouillon
½ pound fresh mushrooms, cleaned and sliced thick
2 tablespoons dry sherry
Standard pastry for 1 crust pie, unbaked
1 egg, beaten

Remove outer membrane of kidney. Split open and remove any fat and white veins. Cut into 1-inch pieces. Soak in salted cold water to cover for 30 minutes. Drain and wipe dry. Dredge kidney and steak cubes with flour, seasoned with salt and pepper. Sauté onion and brown meat cubes, several at a time, on all sides in heated butter in a large saucepan. Gradually add bouillon, stirring as adding, and cook, stirring, until thickened. Cook slowly, covered, 1 hour. Add mushrooms and sherry. Turn into a 2½ quart casserole. Roll out pastry to fit casserole top and fit over dish. Trim and flute edges of pastry, pressing with a fork or the fingers. Make a few slits in top. Brush top with beaten egg. Bake in preheated 425° oven about 20 minutes, until pastry is flaky and golden. Serves 4 to 6.

Salads

Innovative main dish salads from around the world, made with a galaxy of interesting foods, are excellent entrées for luncheons or suppers. Many of them have particular appeal in hot weather for either indoor or outdoor meals.

Although salads have been eaten in most countries from time immemorial, hearty salads, called mixed or composed, are comparatively recent creations. They appeal to the modern cook because they are nutritious, attractive, and easy to prepare and serve.

Mixed salads of several ingredients, termed composed or *grand sallets,* became very popular in Europe during the eighteenth and nineteenth centuries. Court cooks and chefs created exotic combinations with as many as thirty-five ingredients that included not only greens and lettuces but fruits, nuts, flower petals, other vegetables, and a wide range of seasonings. Such dishes were particularly fashionable in Paris as entrées for late evening suppers.

Arranged salads made of contrasting but agreeable foods and

flavorings became especially popular in Scandinavia and Eastern Europe where they are still made with salted and fresh fish, meats, game, and vegetables, and are flavored with piquant foods and dressings.

The early American settlers ate few salads and did not serve them as main dishes. Nutritionists and cookbook writers, however, came to recommend salads for their food values; and American cooks created a wide range of delectable tossed or chef's salads, among others, that became favorite fare in restaurants and homes. Today they are frequently featured as the principal element of memorable meals.

Both mixed green and composed salads can be made with a wide variety of foods and should be carefully prepared so that they appeal not only to the palate but to the eye. The arrangement of the ingredients and display of garnishes play an important role in the preparation of salads.

Choose salad ingredients with care. Every item should be of prime quality and have good texture and color. If greens and lettuces are to be used, select those that are as fresh as possible, crisp looking, and free of blemishes and brown-tipped leaves. Once you have picked or purchased them, wash and dry them carefully. Pat dry with paper toweling, whirl in a wire basket, or use a mechanical spin dryer. Refrigerate at least one hour before using so the greens will be crisp and dry.

Raw or cooked vegetables for salads should be cleaned and refrigerated or cooked shortly before using because exposure to air detracts from their food value and appearance. Don't peel them unless it's necessary. The greatest concentration of vitamins and minerals is in or near the skin. Don't soak them in water because the nutrient elements are soluble and will be lost when the liquid is discarded.

Prepare and cut such foods as meats and poultry so that they are attractive in shape and can be easily handled. Herbs, black and green olives, capers, nuts, and grated cheese will add food value and color to salads.

Salad dressings, preferably made from scratch with only top quality ingredients, should be chosen according to the type of salad. Light oil and vinegar or lemon dressings go well with delicate greens and ingredients. Well-flavored or creamy dressings enhance heartier foods. Dressings made with mayonnaise, sour cream, or yogurt can be used for seafood, meat, or vegetable salads. There are a number of innovative dressings for fruit salads.

Use lemon juice instead of vinegar in dressings if a wine is to be served with the meal.

A hearty mixed green salad to be served as a main dish can be simply made of one or a mixture of greens, raw or cooked vegetables, and some form of protein such as sliced or quartered hard-cooked eggs; strips or cubes of cheese; crumbled Roquefort or blue cheese; diced or flaked cooked fish or shellfish; or julienne cut strips or cubes of poultry or meat.

There is no limit to the possibilities when you're making imaginative main dish salads. You can vary recipes to suit your own tastes and the availability of ingredients. The following international recipes have been designed for home and company meals. A great many of them are superb for entertaining as they are unusual, can most often be partially or totally prepared beforehand, and are convenient and fun to serve. Present as attractively as possible in a large bowl, on a handsome platter, or in a pretty serving dish.

This collection of recipes concentrates on relatively unknown main dish salads from such faraway places as Thailand, Australia, and South Africa. Yet it also includes a few well-known American favorites that have perennial appeal.

South African Curried Chicken Salad

This appealing chicken-fruit salad is attractively served over lettuce leaves. It is a good dish for a weekend brunch.

> *1 cup salad dressing or mayonnaise*
> *3 tablespoons finely chopped chutney*
> *2 teaspoons curry powder*
> *½ teaspoon ground coriander*
> *⅛ teaspoon cayenne*
> *1 small head leafy lettuce, washed, dried and chilled*
> *3 cups diced cooked chicken*
> *1 cup seedless grapes*
> *2 cups pineapple chunks*
> *2 small bananas, sliced*
> *½ cup seedless raisins*
> *2 tablespoons chopped chives*

Combine first five ingredients in a small bowl. Chill 1 to 2 hours to blend flavors. Line a salad bowl with lettuce leaves. Combine chicken, grapes, pineapple, bananas, and raisins with mayonnaise mixture. Spoon over lettuce leaves. Sprinkle top with chives. Serves 6.

Italian Mixed Salad

Chick-peas and zucchini add glamor to this imaginative salad. Serve for an outdoor luncheon or supper.

> *1 quart salad greens, washed, dried, torn into bite-size pieces, and chilled*
> *1 can (1 pound) chick-peas, drained*
> *1 small zucchini, stemmed and sliced*

1 cup mozzarella cheese cubes
¼ pound salami, cut into slivers
1 red onion, peeled, sliced, and separated into rings
1 cup seasoned croutons
1 can (3¾ ounces) sardines in oil, drained
⅓ cup Italian salad dressing

Put salad greens in a large salad bowl. Arrange chick-peas, zucchini, mozzarella, and salami over greens. Top with onion rings, croutons and sardines. Sprinkle with salad dressing just before serving. Serves 4.

Australian Lamb-Rice Salad

This hearty salad can be made with leftover roast lamb and can be prepared beforehand. It is an excellent dinner to serve to company.

1 medium-sized head romaine
3 cups cubed cooked lamb
4 cups cold cooked long grain rice
2 cups cold cooked green peas
1 cup coarsely grated raw carrots
1 medium-sized onion, peeled and minced
3 tablespoons sweet relish
2 cups sour cream
2 tablespoons chopped chives
2 tablespoons fresh lemon juice
1½ teaspoons seasoned salt

Wash and dry romaine; tear into bite-size pieces and refrigerate 1 hour. Line a salad bowl with romaine pieces. Combine lamb, rice, peas, carrots, onion, and relish. Spoon over romaine.

Mix remaining ingredients in a small bowl and serve with salad. Serves 6.

Swedish Shrimp-Macaroni Salad

Prepare this salad with canned or frozen shrimp. It is an attractive main dish for a company summer luncheon.

> 1 package (8 ounces) elbow macaroni, cooked and
>   drained
> 2 cups cleaned, cooked small shrimp
> 1 cup diced celery
> ½ cup diced green peeper
> 2 tablespoons minced dill pickle
> 1 cup sour cream
> 2 tablespoons catsup
> 1 teaspoon dried dillweed
> 1 teaspoon salt
> ¼ teaspoon pepper
> 1 small head leafy lettuce, washed, dried and chilled
> 2 tablespoons chopped chives
> 1 large tomato, peeled and sliced

Combine macaroni, shrimp, celery, green pepper, and pickle in a large bowl. Mix sour cream, catsup, dillweed, salt, and pepper; add to macaroni mixture; mix well. Chill 1 to 2 hours to blend flavors. Arrange lettuce leaves in a salad bowl. Top with macaroni-shrimp mixture. Sprinkle top with chives. Garnish with tomato slices. Serves 4.

Thai Layered Beef-Vegetable Salad

In Thailand this salad is made with beef, vegetables, and exotic native ingredients. You will enjoy this adaptation for an informal dinner.

3 cups shredded lettuce or salad greens, washed, dried, and chilled
1 pound cold, cooked roast beef, cut into bite-size thin strips
1 medium-sized cucumber, peeled and thin sliced
2 medium-sized tomatoes, peeled and thin sliced
1 large carrot, scraped and thin sliced
2 small zucchini, stemmed and thin sliced
2 cloves garlic, crushed
⅓ cup salad oil
3 tablespoons fresh lemon juice
1 tablespoon soy sauce
⅛ teaspoon cayenne
Dash pepper
12 radish roses
2 hard-cooked eggs, shelled and sliced
3 tablespoons chopped fresh coriander or parsley

Put lettuce or greens in a large bowl. Arrange beef strips and vegetables in layers over them. Combine garlic, oil, lemon juice, soy sauce, cayenne, and pepper in a small jar; shake well; pour over salad. Garnish with radishes, eggs, and coriander or parsley. Serves 6.

Spanish Seafood-Rice Salad

This colorful salad is fine for a small luncheon, or you can triple the recipe and serve it for a buffet.

1 can (7 ounces) tuna, drained and broken into chunks
2 cups cooked or canned medium-sized shrimp, cleaned
3 cups cold cooked long grain rice
1 cup chopped green pepper
1 canned pimiento, diced
2 tablespoons capers, drained
½ cup olive oil
3 tablespoons wine vinegar
2 cloves garlic, crushed
1 teaspoon paprika
1½ teaspoons salt
½ teaspoon pepper
1 medium-sized romaine, washed, dried and chilled
1 can (2 ounces) flat anchovies, drained and chopped
½ cup sliced stuffed olives
⅓ cup chopped fresh parsley

Combine first six ingredients in a large bowl. Mix oil, vinegar, garlic, paprika, salt, and pepper in a small jar; shake well, pour over salad, and mix. Chill 1 hour or longer to blend flavors. To serve, arrange romaine leaves in a large bowl. Spoon seafood-rice mixture over them. Garnish with anchovies, olives, and parsley. Serves 4.

West Indies Avocado-Crabmeat Salad

This sour cream flavored crabmeat salad is served in avocado halves and garnished with toasted almonds. Serve for a company weekend luncheon.

½ cup mayonnaise
⅓ cup sour cream
1 tablespoon fresh lemon juice
1 teaspoon grated lemon rind
½ teaspoon ground ginger
2 medium-sized ripe avocados
Juice of 1 lime
1 small head leafy lettuce, washed, dried and chilled
2 cups diced, cleaned, cooked crabmeat
1 cup chopped celery
1 cup seedless grapes
½ cup toasted slivered almonds

Combine first five ingredients. Chill 1 to 2 hours to blend flavors. Halve avocados lengthwise; remove pits, peel, and sprinkle with lime juice. Arrange each half on a bed of lettuce leaves on individual plates. Combine crabmeat, celery, and grapes with mayonnaise mixture. Spoon into avocado halves. Sprinkle with almonds. Serves 4.

Supper Frankfurter-Sauerkraut Salad

This is an appealing entrée for a late evening men's get-together. Or it can be served for a family supper.

¼ cup salad oil
1 medium-sized onion, peeled and chopped
½ pound frankfurters, sliced
1 can (1 pound) sauerkraut, drained
1 medium-sized carrot, scraped and diced

1 medium-sized green pepper, cleaned and diced
⅓ cup tomato sauce
3 tablespoons cider vinegar
½ teaspoon dried thyme
1 teaspoon salt
¼ teaspoon pepper
3 cups diced, cooked, peeled potatoes

Heat oil in a medium-sized skillet. Add onion and frankfurters; cook 10 minutes. Stir in sauerkraut, carrot, green pepper, tomato sauce, vinegar, thyme, salt, and pepper; cook 3 minutes. Add potatoes and leave on stove long enough to heat and blend flavors, about 5 minutes. Remove from heat and serve hot. Serves 4.

Chilean Chicken-Corn Salad

This distinctive salad from Chile is excellent for a summer luncheon.

3 cups cubed cold cooked chicken
2 cups cold cooked fresh or canned whole kernel corn
2 medium-sized green peppers, cleaned and cubed
1 cup sliced radishes
1 medium-sized red onion, peeled and sliced
⅓ cup olive oil
2 tablespoons fresh lemon juice
1 teaspoon salt
¼ teaspoon pepper
Dash cayenne
1 small head leafy lettuce, washed, dried, and chilled
2 hard-cooked eggs, shelled and quartered
2 medium-sized tomatoes, peeled and quartered

Combine first five ingredients in a large bowl. Mix oil, lemon juice, salt, pepper, and cayenne; pour over chicken mixture; mix. Arrange lettuce leaves in a salad bowl or on a platter. Spoon chicken mixture over them. Garnish with eggs and tomatoes. Serves 4.

California Chef's Salad

This version of the well-known chef's salad includes watercress and green peas. It is a good supper entree.

1 clove garlic, halved
1 head romaine, washed, dried, torn into bite-site pieces,
  and chilled
1 head lettuce, washed, dried, torn into bite-size pieces,
  and chilled
1 bunch watercress, washed and dried
½ cup chopped celery
1 medium-sized red onion, peeled, sliced, and separated
  into rings
1 cup cooked green peas
1 small cucumber, peeled and sliced
2 cups cold cooked chicken or turkey strips
2 cups cold cooked ham strips
1 cup slivered Swiss cheese
About ¾ cup French dressing

Rub salad bowl with garlic. Add romaine, lettuce, and watercress; toss. Arrange celery, onion, peas, and cucumber over greens. Top with chicken, ham and cheese. Sprinkle with dressing. Serves 4 to 6.

Dutch Meat-Vegetable Salad

This inviting dish from Holland is called Dutch Hussar's salad. It is superb for a winter luncheon or supper.

2 cups diced cold cooked beef, veal or pork
2 cups diced cold cooked potatoes
1 cup cold cooked green peas
1 medium-sized onion, peeled and diced
2 tablespoons sweet relish
2 hard-cooked eggs, shelled and chopped
1 medium-sized apple, cored and diced
¼ cup salad oil
2 tablespoons wine vinegar
1 teaspoon dried dillweed
1½ teaspoons salt
½ teaspoon pepper
Crisp lettuce leaves, washed, dried and chilled
About ¾ cup mayonnaise
1 medium-sized tomato, peeled and sliced
3 tablespoons chopped fresh parsley

Combine meat, potatoes, peas, onion, relish, eggs, and apple in a large bowl. Mix oil, vinegar, dillweed, salt, and pepper. Add to meat-vegetable mixture; refrigerate 1 to 2 hours to blend flavors. When ready to serve, arrange lettuce leaves on a platter or in a salad bowl. Top with meat-vegetable mixture, shaping into a mound. Cover with a thin coating of mayonnaise. Garnish with tomato slices and parsley. Serves 4.

Summer Fruit-Ham Salad

Serve this colorful salad for a ladies' luncheon.

1 quart shredded salad greens, washed, dried, and
chilled
2 cups cantaloupe cubes
1½ cups halved strawberries
2 cups pineapple chunks
2 cups sliced bananas
1 pound boiled ham, cut into thin strips
½ pound Swiss cheese, cut into thin strips
1½ cups sour cream
3 tablespoons orange juice
1 tablespoon fresh lemon juice
½ teaspoon ground ginger

Line a large salad bowl with shredded greens. Arrange fruit on top. Place ham and cheese strips over fruit. Combine remaining ingredients; pour over salad. Serves 6.

German Sausage-Lentil Salad

This is an inexpensive salad to serve for a winter dinner.

6 cooked frankfurters or Bratwurst sausages, cut into 1-
inch slices
4 cups cold cooked lentils
1 medium-sized onion, peeled and minced
1 large carrot, scraped and diced
¼ cup diced dill pickles
⅓ cup tomato juice

About ¾ cup sour cream
½ teaspoon dried thyme
1½ teaspoons salt
½ teaspoon pepper
2 hard-cooked eggs, shelled and sliced
2 tablespoons chopped fresh dill

Combine frankfurter or Bratwurst slices, lentils, onion, carrot, and pickles in a large bowl. Combine tomato juice, sour cream, thyme, salt, and pepper; pour over sausage-lentil mixture; mix well. Garnish with egg slices and dill. Serves 6 to 8.

Russian Salad Oliver

This well-known chicken and vegetable salad, created by and named for a French chef in the service of Tsar Nicholas II, is elaborately garnished and most attractive. It is marvelous for a company luncheon.

2 cups diced cold cooked white meat of chicken
1 cup diced cold cooked carrots
1 cup cold cooked green peas
2 cups diced cold peeled cooked potatoes
⅓ cup minced dill pickles
6 scallions, cleaned and sliced
½ cup mayonnaise
About ½ cup sour cream
2 tablespoons capers, drained
3 tablespoons chopped fresh dill or 1 teaspoon dried
   dillweed
2 teaspoons salt
½ teaspoon pepper
Crisp lettuce leaves, washed, dried, and chilled

*Garnishes: Cubes of cold cooked lobster, shelled and
cleaned cooked shrimp, hard-cooked egg wedges,
tomato slices, pitted black olives*

Combine chicken, vegetables, pickles, and scallions in a medium-sized bowl. Mix mayonnaise, sour cream, capers, dill, salt, and pepper; add to chicken mixture. Refrigerate 1 hour or longer to blend flavors. To serve, arrange lettuce leaves on a platter or serving dish. Top with salad, shaping as a pyramid or mound. Decorate top and sides and surround with garnishes. Serves 6.

Oriental Beef-Bean Sprout Salad

Tender bean sprouts are combined with vegetables and beef to make this nutritious and colorful salad. It is a good dish for a family supper.

*2 cups cooked beef, cut into thin strips
3 cups bean sprouts, washed and drained
6 scallions, with tops, cleaned and sliced
½ pound fresh mushrooms, cleaned and sliced
1 can (5 ounces) water chestnuts, drained and sliced
1 cup chopped celery
⅓ cup peanut oil
1 tablespoon soy sauce
2 tablespoons rice or white vinegar
2 tablespoons toasted sesame seeds
¼ teaspoon pepper*

Combine first six ingredients in a large bowl; toss. Mix remaining ingredients, pour over salad, and toss. Serves 4 to 6.

Italian Antipasto Salad

This easy to prepare salad can be served for a picnic or home outdoor meal. Prepare beforehand and add dressing just before serving.

> *1 small head leafy lettuce, washed, dried and chilled*
> *½ pound pepperoni, cut into slivers*
> *¼ pound Provolone cheese, cut into cubes*
> *2 hard-cooked eggs, shelled and sliced*
> *1 can (7 ounces) tuna, drained and flaked*
> *8 pitted green or black olives*
> *1 can (2 ounces) flat anchovies, drained*
> *2 medium-sized tomatoes, peeled and cut into wedges*
> *⅓ cup Italian salad dressing*

Arrange lettuce leaves on a platter or in a salad bowl. Top with pepperoni slivers, cheese cubes, egg slices, and tuna. Garnish with olives, anchovies, and tomato wedges. Pour salad dressing over ingredients just before serving. Serves 4.

Polynesian Pork-Sweet Potato Salad

This is a curry flavored hearty salad that is good to serve for a weekend supper.

> *1 small head leafy lettuce, washed, dried and chilled*
> *4 medium-sized sweet potatoes, cooked, peeled and sliced*
> *2 cups cubed cold cooked pork*
> *1 can (1 pound) pineapple chunks, drained*
> *1 medium-sized green pepper, cleaned and cubed*
> *1 small onion, peeled and minced*

1 cup mayonnaise
2 tablespoons pineapple juice
2 teaspoons curry powder
¼ teaspoon paprika
½ cup slivered almonds

Line a salad bowl with lettuce leaves. Place sweet potato slices over them. Combine pork, pineapple, green pepper, and onion; spoon over potatoes. Mix mayonnaise, pineapple juice, curry powder, and paprika; spoon over salad. Sprinkle with almonds. Serves 6.

Salad Niçoise

This well-known salad from southern France is an excellent entrée for a summer luncheon.

4 medium-sized boiled potatoes, peeled and sliced
1½ cups cut up cold cooked green beans
1 large green pepper, cleaned and cut into strips
1 medium-sized red onion, peeled and sliced
2 cans (7 ounces each) tuna, drained and broken into
*   chunks*
⅓ cup olive oil
3 tablespoons wine vinegar
1 tablespoon fresh lemon juice
2 teaspoons sharp prepared mustard
1 teaspoon dried basil
1½ teaspoons salt
½ teaspoon pepper
12 pitted black olives
1 can (2 ounces) flat anchovy fillets, drained and
*   chopped*

3 hard-cooked eggs, shelled and quartered
2 large tomatoes, peeled and quartered

Put first five ingredients in a large bowl. Combine oil, vinegar, lemon juice, mustard, basil, salt, and pepper in a small jar; mix well. Pour over salad; mix. Top with olives, anchovies, eggs, and tomatoes. Refrigerate 1 hour or longer before serving. Serves 6.

Oregon Salmon-Potato Salad

This sour cream and dill flavored salad is handsomely garnished with egg slices and tomato wedges. It is a fine entrée for a company luncheon or supper.

2 cans (1 pound each) salmon
4 cups diced cooked, peeled potatoes
1 cup diced cucumbers
½ cup diced green peppers
1 medium-sized onion, peeled and minced
1 cup mayonnaise
¾ cup sour cream
2 tablespoons fresh lemon juice
1 teaspoon dried dillweed
1½ teaspoons salt
½ teaspoon pepper
1 head leafy lettuce, washed, dried, and chilled
2 hard-cooked eggs, shelled and sliced
2 medium-sized tomatoes, peeled and cut into wedges

Remove skin and bones from salmon; break into chunks. Put with potatoes, cucumber, green pepper, and onion into a large bowl. Combine mayonnaise, sour cream, lemon juice, dillweed, salt, and pepper; add to salmon-potato mixture. Place lettuce leaves on a platter or in a salad bowl and top with salad. Garnish with eggs and tomatoes. Serves 8.

Greek Mixed Salad

This attractive salad features romaine, shrimp, vegetables, and Feta cheese. Serve for a summer luncheon.

*1 medium-sized head romaine, washed, dried, torn into
    bite-size pieces, and chilled*
About ⅓ cup olive oil
6 scallions, cleaned and sliced, with some tops
1 large green pepper, cleaned and cubed
1 medium-sized cucumber, peeled and sliced thin
1 cup sliced radishes
1 pound medium-sized shrimp, cleaned and shelled
3 tablespoons fresh lemon juice
1 teaspoon dried oregano
1½ teaspoons salt
½ teaspoon pepper
12 pitted black olives
1 cup diced Feta cheese
2 medium-sized tomatoes, peeled and cut into wedges
3 tablespoons chopped fresh parsley

Put romaine pieces into a large salad bowl. Add 2 tablespoons oil and toss lightly to coat romaine. Add scallions, green pepper, cucumber, radishes, and shrimp. Combine remaining oil, lemon juice, oregano, salt, and pepper; pour over salad, and toss. Garnish with olives, cheese, tomatoes, and parsley. Serves 6.

Mexican Beef-Taco Salad

This innovative salad from south of the border is a good entrée for a late evening meal. It is attractively garnished with green peppers, olives, and corn chips.

1 pound ground beef
1 medium-sized onion, peeled and minced
2 cloves garlic, crushed
1 can (8 ounces) tomato sauce
2 teaspoons chili powder
1 teaspoon dried oregano
1 teaspoon salt
¼ teaspoon pepper
1 can (1 pound) pinto or kidney beans, drained
1 small head lettuce, washed, dried, and chilled
1 cup shredded Jack or Cheddar cheese
1 cup minced green pepper
½ cup sliced black olives
2 cups packaged corn chips

Cook beef in a medium-sized skillet, mixing with a fork, until redness disappears. Remove any fat. Add onion, garlic, tomato sauce, chili powder, oregano, salt, and pepper. Cook slowly, uncovered, 25 minutes. Remove from heat, mix with beans, and cool. Line a salad bowl with lettuce leaves. Spoon beef-bean mixture over them. Top with cheese, green pepper, olives, and corn chips. Serves 4.

Cape Cod Fish Salad

This nourishing fish-vegetable salad is an inviting entrée for a weekend supper.

1 pound cod or haddock fillets, cooked and cubed
4 cups diced cold cooked potatoes
1 cup chopped green peppers
1 cup chopped celery
½ cup sliced radishes
⅓ cup olive or salad oil

3 *tablespoons fresh lemon juice*
1 *teaspoon dried oregano*
1 *teaspoon salt*
¼ *teaspoon pepper*
4 *large lettuce leaves, washed, dried, and chilled*
2 *tablespoons chopped fresh parsley*

Put fish, potatoes, green pepper, celery, and radishes in a medium-sized bowl. Combine oil, lemon juice, oregano, salt, and pepper. Pour over salad; mix well. Chill 1 to 2 hours to blend flavors. Spoon onto lettuce leaves on four individual plates. Serves 4.

Salade Parisienne

This well-known potato-beef salad is an excellent entrée for an informal dinner.

6 *medium-sized potatoes, washed*
½ *cup dry white wine*
1 *tablespoon wine vinegar*
3 *tablespoons salad oil*
1 *teaspoon dried tarragon*
1½ *teaspoons salt*
¼ *teaspoon pepper*
2 *pounds cold cooked beef or veal, cut into bite-size thin*
   strips
3 *tablespoons minced shallots or scallions*
3 *medium-sized tomatoes, peeled and cut into wedges*
2 *hard-cooked eggs, shelled and sliced*
Crisp lettuce leaves, washed, and dried
1 *medium-sized red onion, peeled, sliced thin, and*
   separated into rings
3 *tablespoons chopped fresh parsley*

Cook potatoes in their jackets in a little salted boiling water until tender, about 25 minutes. Drain, peel, and while still warm, slice into a large bowl. Add wine, vinegar, oil, tarragon, salt, and pepper. Toss lightly. Add beef or veal, shallots, tomatoes, and eggs; toss. Line a salad bowl with lettuce leaves; top with potato-meat mixture; garnish with onion rings and parsley. Serves 6.

Tomato-Tuna Aspic Ring

Serve this colorful molded salad for a ladies' luncheon.

> 2 envelopes unflavored gelatine
> 4 cups tomato juice
> 2 tablespoons cider vinegar
> 1 teaspoon sugar
> ½ teaspoon dried basil
> ½ teaspoon salt
> 2 whole cloves
> 1 bay leaf
> 1 can (7 ounces) flaked tuna
> 1 package (10 ounces) frozen peas, cooked and drained
> ½ cup minced celery
> Dash hot sauce

Sprinkle gelatine on ½ cup cold tomato juice in a medium-sized bowl. Combine remaining 3½ cups tomato juice, vinegar, sugar, basil, salt, cloves, and bay leaf in a medium-sized saucepan. Simmer 5 minutes. Remove and discard cloves and bay leaf. Pour over softened gelatine; stir to dissolve. Chill until partially set. Fold in remaining ingredients and turn into a 6 cup mold. Chill until firm, 5 to 6 hours. Unmold onto a chilled platter. Serves 6.

English Turkey-Macaroni Salad

This inexpensive salad is a good entrée for a family supper.

1 package (8 ounces) elbow macaroni, cooked and
  drained
¼ cup French dressing
2 cups diced cooked turkey
¾ cup diced celery
¼ cup minced onion
2 canned pimientos, drained and chopped
¼ cup minced sweet pickles
About ¼ cup salad dressing or mayonnaise
1 teaspoon salt
¼ teaspoon pepper
Crisp lettuce leaves, washed, dried, and chilled
1 large green pepper, cleaned and cut into rings
1 large tomato, peeled and cut into wedges

Combine warm macaroni with French dressing in a large bowl; mix well. Add turkey, celery, onion, pimientos, and pickles. Mix in salad dressing, enough to bind ingredients. Add salt and pepper. Chill 1 hour or longer to blend flavors. To serve, line a salad bowl with lettuce leaves. Top with salad. Garnish with green pepper and tomato. Serves 4.

Meatballs
and Meat Loaves

Flavorful ground meat mixtures shaped into balls or loaves, served plain or fancy, are among the world's most treasured main dishes. They can be star attractions on buffet tables and are marvelous for informal luncheons and evening meals.

Meatballs and meat loaves were first prepared thousands of years ago when cooks in Southeast Asia and the Middle East discovered that meat, when chopped, scraped or minced, not only cooked more easily and used less fuel, but was more tender and digestible. Combined with grains, spices, or other seasonings, the meat mixtures were found to be more flavorful, went further, and could be fried, cooked on skewers, baked, or simmered in sauces. Ground meat specialties are still staple fare in these areas.

The ancient Greeks combined ground lamb and veal with herbs and bread crumbs to prepare meatballs and loaves which were cooked in piquant sauces. Many of these dishes were adopted by the Romans, who revised the recipes to their tastes. Recipes for meatballs and meat loaves in the world's oldest surviving cookbook by the Roman epicure, Apicius, included minced shellfish, fish, innards, and meats, flavored with spices, sweet-sour sauces, fruits, and nuts.

The Romans introduced the art of making these dishes to other Western European peoples. By the early 1500s a Spanish cookbook listed dozens of recipes for *albondigas,* a name which is still used for meatballs in Spain. The Elizabethan English called them "spoon meat," since before the introduction of forks the food could be easily handled with either a spoon or the fingers. *The Good Hous-Wives Treasurie* of 1588 has recipes for potted meatballs flavored with allspice and *Balles* of *Italie* made with ground veal.

The Germans and other Central Europeans later devised many superb meatball dishes made with their favorite ground pork or veal, or combinations of the two, that generally included piquant flavorings such as capers, lemon juice or vinegar.

French cooks created innovative meat loaves which they called *pains* and which were made with highly seasoned ground mixtures, or forcemeats, of meats, fish, shellfish, game, or vegetables. Such combinations were finely ground or puréed, were baked in pastry or poached in simmering water, and were served either cold or hot. We now call these well-known specialties *pâtés* or terrines. The latter takes its name from the mold or dish in which it is cooked.

Over the years the word *pain* was used less and less for meat loaf and, of course, now means a loaf of bread. Although forcemeat usually indicates a stuffing in culinary terms, the British still refer to meatballs as "forcemeat balls."

The British have long been exceedingly fond of loaves made with "mince" (a colloquialism for ground, or "minced," meat). Their favorites are prepared with well-seasoned combinations of game, pork, veal, and other foods, and are traditionally served either hot or cold not only for home meals but for picnics and in pubs.

North Americans inherited a wealth of meatball and meat loaf recipes from the British and other Europeans as well as from other nationalities. The settlers and immigrants also created their own versions of these dishes with New World foods. Consequently, today we have available to us a superb international collection.

Meatballs and meat loaves can be made with ground beef, veal, pork, lamb, fish, poultry, or liver, combined with stretchers or extenders (bread or cracker crumbs, cereals, etc.), moistening liquids, binders (eggs or egg yolks), and seasonings. Sometimes other foods such as vegetables, cheese, or nuts may also be included.

The meat may be purchased already ground, may be ground by the butcher, or may be ground at home. Sometimes a mixture of two or more kinds of meat is used. Whatever your choice, it is best to use a good grade of meat that is freshly ground, of good color, and which includes at least a modicum of fat.

When combining the meat mixture, handle it as little as possible but enough to thoroughly mix the ingredients. Excessive mixing or kneading will result in less tender food. Mix with your hands or a large spoon.

Meatballs can be made in any size and can be fried, boiled, baked, stewed, or cooked with other foods. They are generally served hot. Meat loaves are shaped into rectangles, rounds or rings, are baked in loaf pans, on cookie sheets, or in rings or molds, and may be topped with sliced bacon, enclosed in pastry, frosted with mashed potatoes, or covered with sauces. They can be served hot or cold.

You will enjoy the following recipes for these ever-appealing specialties.

Mediterranean Meatballs and Vegetables

These meatballs are cooked with eggplant, zucchini, and

tomatoes. They are an attractive and delicious entrée for a small buffet dinner.

> *1 medium-sized eggplant, about 1¼ pounds, stemmed*
>   *and cubed*
> *Salt*
> *1½ pounds ground beef*
> *1 cup Italian seasoned bread crumbs*
> *1½ cups tomato juice*
> *1 egg*
> *½ teaspoon pepper*
> *1 large onion, peeled and sliced*
> *2 cloves garlic, crushed*
> *½ cup salad oil*
> *1 medium-sized zucchini, about ¾ pound, stemmed and*
>   *sliced*
> *1 can (1 pound) tomatoes, chopped*
> *1 teaspoon dried basil*

Put unpeeled eggplant cubes in a colander; sprinkle with salt. Leave 30 minutes to drain. Pat dry with paper toweling. Meanwhile, combine beef, bread crumbs, ½ cup tomato juice, egg, 1½ teaspoons salt, and ¼ teaspoon pepper. Shape into 24 balls and set aside. Sauté onion and garlic in heated oil in an extra large skillet. Add dried eggplant cubes and zucchini slices; sauté 5 minutes. Add tomatoes, remaining 1 cup tomato juice, basil, 1 teaspoon salt, ¼ teaspoon pepper, and meatballs. Cook slowly, covered, 25 minutes, until meatballs and vegetables are cooked. Turn over meatballs once or twice during cooking. Serves 8.

Swiss Meatballs in Cheese Sauce

Pork and ham meatballs cooked in a white wine-cheese sauce are distinctive. Serve for a company luncheon or dinner.

1 pound ground pork
¾ pound ground cooked smoked ham
1¼ cups cracker crumbs
½ cup milk
1 egg
1 medium-sized onion, peeled and minced
2 teaspoons Worcestershire sauce
½ teaspoon dried marjoram
1½ teaspoons salt
¼ teaspoon pepper
2 tablespoons butter or margarine
2 cups dry white wine
1 cup grated Swiss cheese

Combine pork, ham, cracker crumbs, milk, egg, onion, Worcestershire sauce, marjoram, salt, and pepper in a large bowl. Shape into 2-inch balls. Brown in heated butter or margarine on all sides in an extra large skillet. Spoon off any drippings. Add wine and cook slowly, covered, 25 minutes. Add cheese and cook another 10 minutes. Serves 6.

Hungarian Meatballs with Sauerkraut

These pork meatballs are cooked in a savory sauerkraut mixture. They are excellent for a winter supper.

1½ pounds ground pork
1 cup soft rye bread crumbs

½ cup milk
1 egg
1 tablespoon sharp mustard
1 teaspoon dried thyme
1½ teaspoons salt
¼ teaspoon pepper
1 medium-sized onion, peeled and chopped
2 tablespoons salad oil
1 can (1 pound) sauerkraut, drained
2 cups tomato juice
1 medium-sized green pepper, cleaned and chopped
⅓ cup chopped fresh parsley

Combine pork, bread crumbs, milk, egg, mustard, thyme, salt, and pepper in a large bowl. Shape into 2-inch balls. Sauté onion in heated oil in an extra large skillet until tender. Add meatballs and brown on all sides. Add sauerkraut and sauté 2 minutes. Add tomato juice and bring to a boil. Lower heat and cook slowly, covered, 30 minutes, until meatballs are cooked. Add green pepper and parsley 5 minutes before cooking is finished. Serves 6.

Belgian Meatballs in Beer

This is a hearty dish made with meatballs and potatoes in an herb flavored sauce. Serve for a company supper.

2 pounds ground pork or beef
1½ cups soft bread crumbs
½ cup milk
2 eggs, separated
½ cup minced scallions
½ teaspoon ground nutmeg

1½ teaspoons salt
¼ teaspoon pepper
3 tablespoons butter or margarine
1 can (12 ounces) light beer
4 medium-sized potatoes, peeled and quartered
1 bay leaf
½ teaspoon dried thyme
⅓ cup chopped fresh parsley

Combine pork or beef, bread crumbs, milk, egg yolks, scallions, nutmeg, salt, and pepper in a large bowl. Beat egg whites until stiff and fold into meat mixture. Shape into 2-inch balls. Brown on all sides in butter or margarine in a large saucepan. Add remaining ingredients, except parsley, and bring to a boil. Lower heat and cook slowly, covered, 30 minutes, until meatballs and potatoes are cooked. Remove and discard bay leaf. Stir in parsley. Serves 6 to 8.

Greek Meatballs with Egg-Lemon Sauce

These piquant meatballs, called *keftaides avgolemono*, include rice and herbs. Serve for a weekend supper.

1½ pounds ground lamb or beef
½ cup uncooked long grain rice
½ cup minced onion
1 egg
2 tablespoons tomato sauce
¼ cup chopped fresh parsley
½ teaspoon dried oregano
1½ teaspoons salt
¼ teaspoon pepper
2 cups beef bouillon

2 *tablespoons butter or margarine*
3 *egg yolks*
¼ *cup fresh lemon juice*

Combine lamb or beef, rice, onion, egg, tomato sauce, parsley, oregano, salt, and pepper in a large bowl. Shape into 2-inch balls. Bring bouillon to a boil in a large saucepan. Add meatballs and butter and cook slowly, covered, 30 minutes, until meatballs are cooked. Test one to see if rice is tender. Meanwhile, beat egg yolks in a small bowl; stir in lemon juice. Add ½ cup hot liquid; mix well. Add to meatballs, stirring constantly while adding. Leave over low heat about 5 minutes, long enough to thicken a little. Serve at once. Do not reheat. Serves 6.

German Meatballs in Caper Sauce

These piquant meatballs, called *Königsberger Klopse*, originated in the Baltic Sea port city of Königsberg, once a German city but now a part of the USSR. Anchovies, lemon juice, and capers provide a distinctive flavor. Serve for a late evening supper.

2 *pounds ground pork or mixture of pork, veal and beef*
1½ *cups soft bread crumbs*
½ *cup milk*
2 *eggs*
1 *medium-sized onion, peeled and minced*
3 *flat anchovy fillets, drained and minced*
¼ *teaspoon pepper*
4 *cups beef bouillon*
3 *tablespoons butter or margarine*
3 *tablespoons all-purpose flour*
Juice of 1 large lemon

3 tablespoons capers, drained
Salt to taste

Combine pork or meat mixture, bread crumbs, milk, eggs, onion, anchovies, and pepper in a large bowl. Shape into 2-inch balls. Bring bouillon to a boil in a large saucepan; add meatballs. Cook over medium heat, uncovered, until meatballs rise to the top, about 15 minutes. Remove from liquid with a slotted spoon to a pie pan and keep warm. Strain liquid and reserve. Melt butter or margarine in a large saucepan. Stir in flour; blend well. Gradually add 3 cups strained liquid and cook slowly, stirring constantly, until thickened and smooth. Add lemon juice, capers, and meatballs. Season with salt and pepper, if desired. Leave over low heat 5 minutes. Serves 6 to 8.

Mexican Chili Meatballs

These flavorful meatballs can be prepared ahead of time and reheated for a late evening supper. Serve over hot tortillas or tostados, if desired.

1½ pounds ground beef
1 cup yellow cornmeal
½ cup tomato juice
1 egg
1 medium-sized onion, peeled and minced
2 cloves garlic, crushed
1 teaspoon dried oregano
1½ teaspoons salt
¼ teaspoon pepper
2 tablespoons salad oil
1 to 2 tablespoons chili powder
1 can (1 pound) tomatoes, chopped

2 cups canned whole kernel corn, drained
1 large green pepper, cleaned and chopped

Combine beef, cornmeal, tomato juice, egg, onion, garlic, oregano, salt, and pepper in a large bowl. Shape into 24 balls. Heat oil in an extra large skillet. Add chili powder; mix well. Add meatballs and brown on all sides. Add tomatoes and cook slowly, covered, 25 minutes, until meatballs are cooked. Add corn and green pepper 5 minutes, until meatballs are cooked. Add corn and green pepper 5 minutes before cooking is finished. Serves 6.

Russian Meatballs Stroganoff

You can serve these delectable meatballs, cooked in a mushroom-sour cream sauce, for any company meal.

2 pounds ground beef
1½ cups soft rye bread crumbs
½ cup milk
2 eggs
2 tablespoons chopped fresh dill or 1 teaspoon dried
  dillweed
1½ teaspoons salt
¼ teaspoon pepper
1 large onion, peeled and sliced
3 tablespoons salad oil
2 cups beef bouillon
½ pound fresh mushrooms, cleaned and sliced
1 cup sour cream at room temperature
⅓ cup chopped fresh parsley

Combine beef, bread crumbs, milk, eggs, dill or dillweed, salt, and pepper in a large bowl. Shape into 2-inch balls. Sauté onion in heated oil in an extra large skillet. Push aside and brown meatballs on all sides. Add bouillon and bring to a boil. Lower heat and cook slowly, covered, 25 minutes, until meatballs are cooked. Add mushrooms 5 minutes before cooking is finished. Stir in sour cream and parsley and leave on stove a few minutes, long enough to heat through. Serves 8.

Danish Frikadeller

Danes are very fond of meatballs, or *frikadeller,* which are generally made with a combination of pork and veal and served with pickled beets or red cabbage. The meatballs are good for a family dinner.

>*1 medium-sized onion, peeled and minced*
>*4 tablespoons butter or margarine*
>*1 pound ground veal or beef*
>*1 pound ground pork*
>*1¼ cups soft bread crumbs*
>*½ cup milk*
>*2 eggs*
>*1 teaspoon ground allspice*
>*1½ teaspoons salt*
>*¼ teaspoon pepper*
>*⅓ cup chopped fresh parsley*

Sauté onion in 1 tablespoon heated butter or margarine in a small skillet. Combine with meats, bread crumbs, milk, eggs, allspice, salt, and pepper in a large bowl. Shape into slightly flattened 2-inch balls. Pan fry on both sides in remaining heated butter over medium heat. Add a little water and simmer, covered, 15 minutes, until cooked. Garnish with parsley. Serves 6 to 8.

Oriental Sweet and Sour Meatballs

These meatballs simmer in a tangy sauce which includes pineapple, green peppers, and fresh ginger. You can serve them alone or with hot rice or egg noodles for a nourishing family supper.

1½ pounds ground beef
1 cup soft bread crumbs
⅓ cup water
1 egg
1 medium-sized onion, peeled and minced
1 tablespoon soy sauce
2 to 3 teaspoons curry powder
¼ teaspoon pepper
2 tablespoons peanut oil
2 tablespoons cornstarch
3 tablespoons cider vinegar
3 tablespoons soy sauce
1 cup beef bouillon
1 can (15½ ounces) pineapple chunks
1 teaspoon minced fresh ginger
1 large green pepper, cleaned and cubed

Combine beef, bread crumbs, water, egg, onion, soy sauce, curry powder, and pepper in a large bowl. Shape into 24 balls. Brown on all sides in heated oil in an extra large skillet. Combine cornstarch, vinegar, soy sauce, bouillon, and juice of pineapple chunks. Add to meatballs; mix well. Cook slowly, covered, 25 minutes, until meatballs are cooked. Stir occasionally during cooking. Add pineapple chunks, ginger, and green pepper 5 minutes before cooking is finished. Serves 6.

Baked Veal Meatballs and Rice

This hearty dish is an excellent entrée for a weekend dinner.

1½ pounds ground veal
1 cup Italian seasoned bread crumbs
½ cup milk
1 egg
2 cloves garlic, crushed
1½ teaspoons salt
¼ teaspoon pepper
1 large onion, peeled and chopped
2 large green peppers, cleaned and chopped
¼ cup butter or margarine
1 can (1 pound) tomatoes, chopped
3 cups cooked long grain rice
⅓ cup chopped fresh parsley

Combine veal, bread crumbs, milk, egg, garlic, salt, and pepper in a large bowl. Shape into 2-inch balls. Melt butter in a 13×9×2-inch baking dish in a 400° oven. Add onion and peppers and bake 10 minutes. Remove from oven and arrange tomatoes, rice, and meatballs over onion-pepper mixture. Sprinkle with parsley. Return to oven and bake 45 minutes, until meatballs are cooked. Serves 8.

Swedish Smorgasbord Meatballs

You can serve these spice flavored meatballs in a chafing dish for a buffet or dinner.

4 slices stale white bread
⅔ cup light cream or milk

2½ pounds meat loaf mixture or ground beef
2 eggs
1 medium-sized onion, peeled and minced
½ teaspoon ground nutmeg
1 teaspoon ground allspice
2 teaspoons salt
½ teaspoon pepper
4 tablespoons salad oil
2 cups beef bouillon
¼ cup butter or margarine
¼ cup all-purpose flour
1 cup sour cream, at room temperature
⅓ cup chopped fresh dill

Soak bread slices in cream or milk in a large bowl. Mash with a fork. Add meat, eggs, onion, nutmeg, allspice, salt, and pepper. Shape into 2-inch balls. Brown in heated oil on all sides in an extra large skillet. Add bouillon and bring to a boil. Lower heat and cook slowly, covered, 30 minutes. Remove with a slotted spoon to a pie pan and keep warm. Strain liquid and reserve. Melt butter in a large saucepan. Add flour and cook 1 minute to blend well. Gradually add strained liquid and cook slowly, stirring, until smooth and thick. Add meatballs and leave on stove long enough to become hot. Stir in sour cream and dill and leave over low heat 5 minutes. Serves 8 to 10.

Italian Meatballs in Tomato Sauce

These meatballs are a good dish for a family or company dinner.

1½ pounds ground beef or mixture of pork, veal and beef
1 cup fresh bread crumbs
½ cup milk

1 egg
2 teaspoons salt
½ teaspoon pepper
3 tablespoons olive or salad oil
1 large onion, peeled and minced
2 cloves garlic, crushed
2 cans (1 pound each) tomatoes, chopped
¼ cup tomato paste
1 teaspoon dried oregano
⅛ cup chopped fresh parsley

Combine meat, bread crumbs, milk, egg, 1½ teaspoons salt, and ¼ teaspoon pepper in a large bowl. Shape into 2-inch balls. Brown on all sides in heated oil in an extra large skillet. Remove from pan to a plate. Add onion and garlic to drippings; sauté until tender. Add tomatoes, tomato paste, oregano, remaining ½ teaspoon salt, and ¼ teaspoon pepper. Cook slowly, uncovered, stirring occasionally, 15 minutes. Add meatballs and cook 25 minutes longer. Mix in parsley. Serves 6.

Russian Stuffed Meat Loaf

This innovative meat loaf is stuffed with cooked rice, eggs, and dillweed, and can be served with tomato sauce, if desired. It is a good entrée for a company dinner.

2 slices whole wheat bread
½ cup milk
2 pounds ground beef
1 medium-sized onion, peeled and minced
⅓ cup chopped fresh parsley
1½ teaspoons salt
¼ teaspoon pepper
2 cups cooked long grain rice

2 hard-cooked eggs, shelled and chopped
1 teaspoon dried dillweed

Soak bread in milk in a medium-sized bowl until soft. Mash with a fork. Add beef, onion, parsley, salt, and pepper; mix well. Pack half of beef mixture into a lightly greased 9×5×3-inch loaf pan. Make an indentation lengthwise along center of beef mixture. Combine rice, eggs, and dillweed. Spoon into indentation. Top with remaining beef mixture. Shape into a loaf, completely enclosing filling. Bake in a preheated 350° oven 1 hour, until loaf shrinks from edges of pan. Spoon off drippings. Transfer to a serving dish with two broad spatulas. Cut into slices to serve. Serve with tomato sauce, if desired. Serves 6.

Old-Fashioned Mixed Meat Loaf

Everyone enjoys this old time favorite herb flavored meat loaf which is topped with bacon slices.

2 pounds meat loaf mixture (beef, veal and pork)
1 cup soft bread crumbs
½ cup milk
½ cup minced onions
½ cup minced celery
2 eggs, beaten
½ cup chopped fresh parsley
1 teaspoon dried herbs (savory, basil, sage, or marjoram)
1½ teaspoons salt
¼ teaspoon pepper
3 slices thin bacon

Combine ingredients, except bacon, in a large bowl. Pack into a lightly greased 9×5×3-inch loaf pan. Top with bacon slices.

Bake in a preheated 350° oven 1 hour, until loaf shrinks slightly from edges of pan. Spoon off drippings. Transfer to a serving dish with two broad spatulas. Cut into slices to serve. Serves 6.

New England Salmon Loaf

This traditional loaf is flavored with capers and lemon juice. It is a good dish for a ladies' luncheon.

> 1 can (1 pound) salmon, cleaned and flaked
> 2 cups soft bread crumbs
> ½ cup milk
> 2 eggs, beaten
> 1 medium-sized onion, peeled and minced
> 2 teaspoons capers, drained
> 2 tablespoons fresh lemon juice
> ½ teaspoon crumbled dried rosemary
> ½ cup chopped fresh parsley
> 1½ teaspoons salt
> ¼ teaspoon pepper
> 2 cups hot cooked green peas

Combine ingredients, except peas, in a large bowl. Pack into a lightly greased 9×5×3-inch loaf pan. Bake in a preheated 350° oven 45 minutes, until loaf is cooked. Transfer to a serving dish with two broad spatulas. Surround with green peas. Cut into slices to serve. Serves 6.

Danish Veal-Pork Loaf

Pickled beets add a piquant flavor to this meat loaf which is garnished with cucumber slices and chopped dill. Serve for a Sunday night supper.

1 pound ground veal
1 pound ground pork
1 cup fine dry bread crumbs
½ cup milk
2 eggs, beaten
1 medium-sized onion, peeled and minced
1 cup minced pickled beets
⅓ cup chopped fresh parsley
1½ teaspoons salt
¼ teaspoon pepper
1 medium-sized cucumber, peeled and sliced
2 tablespoons chopped fresh dill

Combine ingredients, except cucumbers and dill, in a large bowl. Pack into a lightly greased 9×5×3-inch loaf pan. Bake in preheated 350° oven 1¼ hours, until loaf shrinks from edges of pan. Spoon off drippings. Transfer to a serving dish with two broad spatulas. Garnish with cucumber slices sprinkled with dill. Cut into slices to serve. Serves 6.

Swedish Meat Loaf with Mushrooms

You will want to serve this attractive meat loaf for a company meal. It is stuffed and garnished with mushrooms.

1 cup sliced scallions, with some tops
2 cups sliced fresh mushrooms
2 tablespoons butter or margarine
½ cup sour cream
2 pounds ground beef
½ cup beef bouillon
1 cup fine dry bread crumbs
1 teaspoon prepared horseradish
2 tablespoons chopped fresh dill or 1 teaspoon dried dillweed

1½ teaspoons salt
¼ teaspoon pepper
½ cup chopped fresh parsley

Sauté scallions and 1 cup mushrooms in heated butter or margarine in a small skillet 4 minutes. Remove from heat; mix in sour cream. Combine remaining ingredients, except parsley, in a large bowl. Put half of beef mixture into a lightly greased 9×5×3-inch loaf pan. Make an indentation lengthwise along center of beef. Spoon mushroom mixture into indentation. Top with remaining beef mixture. Shape into a loaf, completely enclosing filling. Bake in a preheated 350° oven 1 hour, until loaf shrinks from edges of pan. Spoon off drippings. Transfer to a serving dish with two broad spatulas. Garnish top with remaining cup of sliced mushrooms and parsley. Cut into slices to serve. Serves 6.

German Sausage Ring Loaf with Sauerkraut

This is an exceptional loaf which is stuffed with sauerkraut, green peppers, and carrots. Serve for a weekend dinner.

2 cups finely chopped drained sauerkraut
½ cup minced green peppers
½ cup minced raw carrots
2 pounds bulk pork sausage meat
1 cup fine dry bread crumbs
1 egg, beaten
½ cup minced onions
⅓ cup tomato juice
¾ teaspoon dried thyme
1½ teaspoons salt
¼ teaspoon pepper
1 cup parsley sprigs, washed and dried

Combine sauerkraut, peppers, and carrots in a small bowl. Mix remaining ingredients, except parsley, in a large bowl. Put half of sausage mixture into a lightly greased 6-cup ring mold. Top with sauerkraut mixture, spreading evenly. Cover with remaining sausage mixture; pack firmly. Place filled mold on a baking sheet. Bake in a preheated 350° oven 1¼ hours, until loaf shrinks from edges of pan. Spoon off drippings twice during cooking. Remove from oven and spoon off all drippings. Cool. Invert serving plate on top of mold. Holding plate and mold together, turn right side up. Gently remove mold. Place parsley in center. Cut into slices to serve. Serves 8.

New Hampshire Vegetable-Meat Loaf

This nourishing meat loaf is a good entrée for a family supper.

2 pounds ground pork or beef
2 cups grated raw carrots
1 cup minced green peppers
½ cup minced onions
1 cup crumbled crackers
½ cup milk
2 eggs, beaten
½ teaspoon dried sage
½ cup chopped fresh parsley
1½ teaspoons salt
¼ teaspoon pepper

Combine ingredients in a large bowl. Pack into a lightly greased 9×5×3-inch loaf pan. Bake in a preheated 350° oven 1 hour, until loaf shrinks from edges of pan. Spoon off drippings. Transfer to a serving dish with two broad spatulas. Cut into slices to serve. Serves 6.

Turkish Lamb Loaf

This lamb loaf has a center of hard-cooked eggs and is garnished with tomato wedges. You can serve it for a dinner or double the recipe to make two loaves for a buffet.

1½ pounds ground lamb
½ pound ground beef
1 cup soft bread cubes
½ cup tomato juice
2 cloves garlic, crushed
1 medium-sized onion, peeled and minced
1 cup minced green pepper
1 teaspoon ground allspice
½ cup chopped fresh parsley
1½ teaspoons salt
¼ teaspoon pepper
2 hard-cooked eggs, shelled
2 medium-sized tomatoes, peeled and cut into wedges

Combine ingredients, except hard-cooked eggs and tomatoes, in a large bowl. Flatten into a rectangle on a baking sheet. Place eggs lengthwise along center. Fold meat mixture around eggs to completely enclose them and to form a loaf. Bake in a preheated 350° oven 1 hour, until loaf shrinks from edges of pan. Spoon off any accumulated drippings during and after cooking. Transfer to a serving dish with two broad spatulas. Cut into slices to serve. Garnish with tomatoes. Serves 6.

Pastry-Covered Curried Loaf

A flaky pastry covering adds elegance to this curry flavored meat loaf. Serve for a weekend brunch or luncheon.

2 pounds meat loaf mixture (beef, veal, and pork)
1 cup soft bread crumbs
½ cup hot beef bouillon
½ cup minced onions
2 eggs, beaten
1 tablespoon Worcestershire sauce
1 tablespoon curry powder
1½ teaspoons salt
¼ teaspoon pepper
2 sticks piecrust mix
1 egg yolk beaten with 1 tablespoon water

Combine meat, bread crumbs, bouillon, onions, eggs, Worcestershire sauce, curry powder, salt, and pepper in a large bowl. Pack into a lightly greased 9×5×3-inch loaf pan. Bake in a preheated 350° oven 1 hour, until loaf shrinks from edges of pan. Spoon off drippings. Transfer to a baking sheet with two broad spatulas. Cool. Prepare piecrust mix to make pastry for a 2-crust pie. Roll into a 10×14-inch rectangle. Place cooled meat loaf in center of rectangle. Fold pastry around loaf and seal edges with water. Turn upright and place on a baking sheet. Brush with egg yolk and water. Bake in a preheated 425° oven 12 minutes, until pastry is golden and flaky. Transfer to a serving dish with two broad spatulas. Cut into slices to serve. Serves 6.

English Picnic Loaf

You will enjoy this loaf for an outdoor meal or picnic. It is good whether served hot, lukewarm, or cold.

2 pounds bulk pork sausage meat
1 medium-sized onion, peeled and minced
½ cup minced carrot
½ cup diced celery

3 eggs, beaten
2 tablespoons Worcestershire sauce
3 tablespoons sweet pickle relish
1½ teaspoons salt
¼ teaspoon pepper
½ cup macaroni elbows
¼ cup chopped fresh parsley

Cook sausage meat over low heat, mixing with a fork, in a medium-sized skillet until redness disappears. Drain off all but ¼ cup of fat. Remove sausage to a large bowl. Add onion, carrot, and celery to remaining fat and sauté 5 minutes. Add to sausage; mix well. Stir in eggs, Worcestershire sauce, relish, salt, and pepper. Cook macaroni until tender; drain. Add, with parsley, to sausage mixture; mix thoroughly. Pack into a lightly greased 9×5×3-inch loaf pan. Bake in a preheated 350° oven 30 minutes, until loaf is cooked. Transfer to a serving dish with two broad spatulas. Cut into slices to serve. Serve hot or cold. Serves 6 to 8.

Connecticut Ham Loaf with Mustard Sauce

This old-time Connecticut loaf can be made with leftover cooked smoked ham. It is served with a piquant mustard sauce. You will enjoy the loaf for a weekend luncheon.

2 pounds ground cooked smoked ham (about 5 cups)
1 medium-sized onion, peeled and minced
1 cup fine dry bread crumbs
2 eggs, beaten
½ cup milk
½ teaspoon dried basil
½ teaspoon salt
Dash pepper

Combine ingredients in a large bowl. Pack into a lightly greased 9×5×3-inch loaf pan. Bake in a preheated 350° oven 1 hour. Transfer to a serving dish with two broad spatulas. Cut into slices to serve. Serve with Mustard Sauce (recipe below). Serves 6.

Mustard Sauce

1 cup light cream
1 teaspoon dry mustard
⅓ cup sugar
1 tablespoon all-purpose flour
⅓ cup cider vinegar
1 teaspoon salt
⅛ teaspoon pepper
1 egg yolk

Combine ingredients, except egg yolk, in top of a double boiler. Heat over simmering water, stirring, until slightly thickened. Spoon some of hot sauce over egg yolk in a small bowl; mix well. Return to sauce and cook, stirring, until thick and smooth. Serve hot.

Dilled Tuna Ring Mold

This colorful tuna loaf is a good choice for a ladies' luncheon. It is served with a sour cream-cucumber sauce.

1½ cups sour cream
¼ cup chopped scallions, with some tops
1 cup chopped cucumbers
½ teaspoon dried dillweed
1 teaspoon salt

2 cans (7 ounces each) tuna, drained and flaked
1 cup fine dry bread crumbs
2 eggs, beaten
½ cup minced onion
1 cup minced green pepper
1 can (10½ ounces) condensed cream of celery soup
Dash pepper

Combine 1 cup sour cream, scallions, cucumbers, dillweed, and ½ teaspoon salt in a small bowl; chill. Combine tuna, bread crumbs, eggs, ½ cup sour cream, onion, green pepper, celery soup, ½ teaspoon salt, and pepper in a large bowl. Turn into a lightly greased 5-cup ring mold. Bake in a preheated 350° oven 50 minutes, or until cooked. Invert on a serving plate on top of mold. Holding plate and mold together, turn right side up. Gently remove mold. Cut into slices to serve. Serve with chilled sour cream-cucumber sauce. Serves 4 to 6.

Near Eastern Lamb-Cracked Wheat Loaf

The national dish of Lebanon and Syria called *kibbeh* consists of lamb ground to a paste with cracked wheat (bulgur) and seasonings. It may be molded into a ball and served either raw or deep fried, or formed into a loaf and baked. Traditionally it is made by pounding the ingredients in a stone or metal mortar with a heavy pestle. This is one variation that can be easily made in the home kitchen.

1½ cups cracked wheat (bulgur)
1½ pounds lean ground lamb
½ teaspoon ground nutmeg
½ teaspoon ground allspice or cinnamon
1½ teaspoons salt

¼ teaspoon pepper
3 tablespoons chopped pine nuts
5 tablespoons butter or margarine
1 medium-sized onion, peeled and minced
⅓ cup chopped fresh parsley

Soak cracked wheat in water to cover for 30 minutes. Squeeze dry and combine with lamb, spices, salt, and pepper in a bowl. Turn out on a flat surface and work with the hands to thoroughly combine ingredients. Sauté pine nuts in 3 tablespoons butter or margarine for 1 minute. Spoon into a bowl with a slotted spoon. Sauté onion in drippings until tender. Mix with pine nuts. Spread half of lamb mixture in a shallow round baking dish or pie plate. Top with sautéed pine nuts, onions, and butter drippings, spreading evenly. Spread with remaining half of lamb mixture. Dip the tip of a knife in cold water and cut lines diagonally across the top to make diamond shapes. Bake in a preheated 350° oven 30 minutes. Remove from oven and pour off any fat that has accumulated. Spread top with remaining 2 tablespoons butter or margarine and put in a 450° oven 10 minutes. Sprinkle top with parsley. Serve hot or cold and with plain yogurt, if desired. Serves 6.

Curries

Creative curries are made to order for entertaining. Because they improve with age, you can prepare them in advance and simply reheat at mealtime. Curries are attractive and different and may be served at the dining table for a few persons, or buffet style to a larger number of guests.

The culinary preparation that has become known as a curry has a magical connotation long associated with the colorful East. There is also considerable mystery concerning what a curry actually is and its varied role on international menus.

The English term curry derives from the Tamil word *kari* meaning "sauce," which in India would be richly spiced. Curry, however, has never been the name of a particular dish in India nor is the name used traditionally by Indians to describe any food preparation.

Before the arrival in India of European soldiers and traders in the 1600s, there were no specific dishes called curries. Neither did a curry powder exist. As far as is known, curry became a catchall word used by the British, and passed on to other nationalities, to describe a wide range of foods cooked in spicy sauces.

For thousands of years before then, Indians had been utilizing a wide variety of native spices, herbs, and seeds, grown in abundance in their wet and humid climate, to flavor their foods. The plant parts were ground into powders with mortar and pestle and cooks developed the art of making the best combinations to suit certain foods—meats, poultry, seafood, vegetables, and eggs. The spices provided flavor, color, aroma, and pungency. This is still the practice today.

Over the years the Indian art of preparing and cooking food with spices spread to neighboring countries, and the spicy stewlike dishes eventually became known in many lands as curries. Most of the best versions are still prepared in fascinating variety, as they have been for centuries, for daily meals in the countries of Southeast Asia—India, Pakistan, Sri Lanka (Ceylon), Burma, Thailand, Malaysia, and Indonesia.

Thanks to British colonists and the clipper ships of the nineteenth century, curries became popular in Western countries. The British also began blending and packaging Indian spices to make curry powders, and thus introduced European and American versions of curries which are still thickly sauced dishes featuring seafood, poultry, or meat.

The so-called curries of India cover a wide range of dishes from many regions. They are mild, hot, or in-between. Some are sweet, some sour. They are made in various colors ranging from pale yellow to green and deep red, and can be wet (richly sauced) or dry (without sauce). The foods may be left whole, cut into large pieces or chunks, sliced, or formed into balls.

There are hundreds of varieties of curries. Each locale has its own specialties. Local climates, ingredients, religions, and inherited tastes determine the selection. For example, in the temperate northern locales curries tend to be fairly mild and sweet or fragrant due to such spices as cinnamon, cloves, nutmeg, and mace. In the hotter southern areas the curries are made more spicy with green chilis and red peppers (introduced from America in the seventeenth century) and are also flavored with tropical fruits and coconut.

Among the best known kinds of Indian curries are *kormas* (dry curries made of foods marinated and cooked in spiced yogurt); *koftas* (made of finely ground meat or poultry shaped into balls and cooked in sauces); *kababs* (pieces of food threaded on skewers and grilled); *vindaloos* (sour or tart curries made of foods cooked in a well-spiced vinegar sauce); *pulaos* (dry rice and meat or poultry curries flavored with whole spices); and *biryanis* (elaborate rice and meat, poultry or seafood curries garnished with several colorful foods).

Southeast Asian curries are too numerous and varied to mention in detail. The Burmese favor strong and fragrant down-to-earth curries. Nepal has curries made with buffalo and goat meat. Ceylonese, Malaysian, and Indonesian curries span a wide range of flavors and colors and include such favorite native foods as lemon grass, fish sauce, and curry leaf, as well as chilis, sweet and pungent spices, and coconut milk or shredded coconut.

Thailand's curries, made with traditional home-ground powders and pastes, are especially interesting. In addition to the commonly used Eastern spices, they are flavored with aromatic leaves and herbs, shrimp paste, tamarind, and coconut milk, besides other exotic flavorings. Some are mellow and fragrant, but among the best curries are those which are very hot and fiery due to the liberal use of chilis.

The British, as well as the Australians and New Zealanders, and, of course, the Americans, have developed their own versions of curries that are made with a wide variety of foods, and flavored primarily with bland curry powder.

East Indian and Malaysian colonists and workers introduced curries to East and South Africa, where they play a substantial role in the cookery. Some of the dishes are similar to the native Eastern ones, but many are intriguing adaptations featuring local meats and game. Curries are also enjoyed in the Caribbean islands, where they are enhanced with tropical fruits and flavorings.

Eastern curries are prepared with freshly ground spices and may include only a few or many. Cooks use different spice blends in varying proportions for each dish. These are generally mixed according to family formulas. The mixtures provide texture as well as flavor, and thicken and color the dishes. The Indian *garam masala,* a special blend of spices, herbs, and perhaps other seasonings, is a dry mixture that may be either mild and delicate or strong and sharp. When liquid is added to the mixture it becomes a wet *masala.*

Nearly all of the Eastern curry blends include several of the same basic spices. Among the best known are caraway seed, cardamon, cinnamon, cloves, cumin, fenugreek, chilis, ginger, black and white pepper, mustard seeds, poppy seeds, and turmeric. Each gives a particular quality to the mixture. For example, cloves add an aromatic perfume. Poppy seeds are rich in oil and act as thickening agents. Ginger provides a subtle flavor. Green chilis give a green color, and red chilis a red tint.

Westerners can grind or mix their own *garam masalas* or other curry blends in the home, if desired. But it is not always advisable unless you know the right combinations and have high quality products. All spices should be fresh. While many kinds of spices are available in our stores, some such as asafetida, fenugreek, white poppy seeds, and black mustard seeds, are difficult to find.

Ideally, the spices should be ground or pounded by hand with a mortar and pestle. You can, however, use a spice or coffee grinder. Or, for a larger quantity, an electric blender is practicable.

Prepared *garam masala* and other Eastern dry spice mixtures and pastes can be purchased in Indian and Oriental food stores or specialty groceries and are well worth seeking to make curries at home.

You can also use commercial curry powder, if you wish. Curry powder, a blend of several spices, will vary according to the type as well as the manufacturer. It ranges generally from golden yellow to yellow-brown in color and may be mild or hot. Madras curry powders and pastes are noted for their hotness. Curry pastes, also made with a blend of spices, as well as oil, and perhaps vinegar, are stronger than powders. Most commercial blends have a preponderance of turmeric, the root of an East Indian plant of the ginger family, which accounts for the golden color of the powder or paste.

When making curries, some Western cooks prefer to use a commercial mild curry and to add ginger and/or chilis or other spices to enhance the flavor and make it hotter. Garlic, fresh herbs, and perhaps grated fruit rinds, are also good additions.

All curry powders and pastes, whether homemade or purchased, should be a perfect blend so that no particular spice is so strong that it will dominate the dish. They also must be cooked in a small amount of heated fat or oil before other foods are added so that the flavor is developed. Otherwise the dish will have an undesirable raw taste.

Indians use ghee, clarified butter, or oils such as vegetable, coconut or mustard oil to make curries. Peanut oil is a good bland oil. Onions and/or garlic, and perhaps other seasonings, are sautéed or fried in the oil before the main ingredients are added. For best results, curries should be made with fresh meat, poultry, or seafood, rather than leftovers.

Various liquids may be used in making curries. A very popular one is coconut milk or cream, made by soaking grated coconut meat in boiling water, and then straining and squeezing it to produce a thick liquid. It can be made in the home or purchased in most Eastern groceries. The milk or cream is used for flavoring and thickening the curry. When added to the dish, it is cooked uncovered.

Eastern curries are never thickened with flour or cornstarch. If the sauce is too thin it can be thickened with coconut milk, grated coconut or yogurt, or reduced by cooking uncovered. Tart fruit juices or fruits provide pleasing acid flavors to many curries.

Curries are cooked slowly in a heavy deep skillet or an Oriental wok, if desired, for at least 30 minutes and sometimes quite a bit longer to blend the flavors and develop the proper consistency. A good curry tastes better if made one or two days before it is served to allow the flavors to develop or "season."

Eastern curries are not served, as in the West, with many condiments sprinkled on top. They are usually served plain, or with one or two pickles or chutneys made with limes, lemons, mangoes, or other fruits. Fresh chutneys, made with fresh coriander leaves, mint, parsley, coconut, onions, tomatoes, and yogurt, or sweet ones, made of fruits, are good accompaniments. Rice is also served with most curries, except those which are prepared with rice.

The following collection of international curries has been selected for Western tastes. The recipes for most Eastern curries are adaptations. You will find them all interesting to make and fun to serve. While most are for a few persons, the recipes can be doubled or tripled. For a larger group or more elaborate presentation, serve several curries at one time.

Malaysian Beef Curry

This a good curry for a small dinner party.

2 cloves garlic, crushed
1 teaspoon minced fresh ginger
½ cup chopped onions
1 tablespoon ground coriander
1 tablespoon chili powder
1 tablespoon ground turmeric
3 tablespoons salad oil
2 pounds boneless beef, cut into 1-inch cubes
1 cup beef bouillon or water
1 cup coconut milk
2 teaspoons brown sugar
1 teaspoon ground cinnamon
2 tablespoons fresh lemon juice

Mash garlic, ginger, onions, coriander, chili powder, and turmeric with a little water to make a thick paste, or whirl in a blender. Fry in heated oil in a large deep skillet for 2 to 3 minutes. Wipe beef cubes dry and brown in oil on all sides. Add bouillon and cook slowly, covered, 45 minutes to 1 hour. Add remaining ingredients and cook, uncovered, about 30 minutes, until meat is tender. The exact time will depend on the kind of beef used, less for more tender cuts. Serves 6.

Pakistan Chicken Curry

This curry features chicken cooked in a spicy yogurt sauce. Serve for a luncheon.

1 broiler-fryer chicken, about 2½ pounds, cut up
2 large onions, peeled and sliced thin
3 tablespoons salad oil
3 cloves garlic, crushed
1 tablespoon ground coriander
1 tablespoon ground turmeric
½ teaspoon ground ginger
4 whole cloves
¼ teaspoon ground red pepper
2 bay leaves
Salt to taste
About 2 tablespoons water
1 cup plain yogurt
¼ cup chopped fresh coriander or mint

Remove skin from chicken. Cut large pieces into several smaller pieces. Pat dry with paper toweling. Sauté onions in heated oil in a large deep skillet until tender. Push aside. Add garlic, coriander, turmeric, ginger, cloves, red pepper, bay leaves, and salt. Cook 2 minutes. Add chicken pieces and fry on all sides, turning with tongs, until golden. Add water and yogurt. Cook slowly, covered, about 40 minutes, until chicken is tender. Add a little more water, if needed. The finished sauce should be thick and creamy. Remove and discard cloves and bay leaves. Serve sprinkled with coriander or mint. Serves 4 to 6.

Kashmir Meatball Curry

In India meatballs made of a mixture of ground or minced meat and spices are called *koftas*. When cooked in a gravy or sauce the dish is called a *kofta* curry. This is a simplified version. Serve as an entrée for a late evening meal.

2 pounds ground lamb or beef
1½ cups plain yogurt
1½ teaspoons salt
1 tablespoon ground coriander
1 teaspoon ground cumin
1 teaspoon ground cardamom
¼ teaspoon each of ground cinnamon, nutmeg, and
  cloves
1 teaspoon ground ginger
½ teaspoon pepper
4 tablespoons clarified butter or salad oil
2 teaspoons ground red pepper
½ cup chopped fresh coriander or parsley

Combine lamb or beef with ¼ cup yogurt and salt in a large bowl. Fry spices in 1 tablespoon heated butter or oil in a small skillet for 2 minutes. Add to meat mixture; mix well. Shape into 1½-inch balls. Brown in remaining 3 tablespoons heated butter or oil on all sides in a large deep skillet. Add red pepper and remaining 1¼ cups yogurt; mix well. Cook slowly, tightly covered, about 30 minutes, until meatballs are cooked. Serve sprinkled with coriander. Serves 6 to 8.

Burmese Shrimp-Tomato Curry

This is an elegant curry to serve for a ladies' luncheon.

1 large onion, peeled and minced
4 cloves garlic, minced
2 teaspoons ground turmeric
1 teaspoon ground dried chili peppers
¼ teaspoon pepper
2 tablespoons salad oil

2 pounds uncooked shelled and deveined shrimp
2 tablespoons fish or soy sauce
2 large tomatoes, peeled and chopped

Sauté onion, garlic, turmeric, chili peppers, and pepper in heated oil in a large skillet 3 minutes. Add remaining ingredients and cook slowly, covered, about 10 minutes, until shrimp are pink and tender. Remove shrimp to a warm serving dish. Reduce sauce until thickened. Pour over shrimp. Serves 4 to 6.

Martinique Chicken Colombo

Colombos are a curry specialty of northern Martinique, where they were introduced by East Indian workers. These curries generally include several tropical fruits and vegetables and are flavored with tamarind, a sour brown fruit. Serve for a weekend luncheon.

1 broiler-fryer chicken, about 2½ pounds, cut up
3 tablespoons peanut or salad oil
2 medium-sized onions, peeled and chopped
2 cloves garlic, crushed
2 to 3 tablespoons curry powder, preferably Madras
½ teaspoon ground red pepper
1½ teaspoons salt
½ teaspoon pepper
1 cup chicken broth
1 medium-sized eggplant, peeled and cubed
½ pound Hubbard squash, peeled and cubed
1 mango, peeled and chopped
1 cup coconut milk
Juice of 1 lime

Remove skin from chicken pieces. Cut larger pieces into smaller pieces. Pat dry with paper toweling. Fry in heated oil on all sides in a large deep skillet. Remove with tongs to a plate. Add onions, garlic, curry powder, red pepper, salt, and pepper to drippings; sauté 3 or 4 minutes. Return chicken pieces to skillet. Add chicken broth, eggplant, and squash. Cook slowly, covered, 30 minutes. Add mango, coconut milk, and lime juice and cook, uncovered, about 20 minutes, until ingredients are cooked. Mix occasionally while cooking. Serves 4 to 6.

Indonesian Chicken Curry

This piquant curry includes potatoes. Serve for a dinner.

> *3 pounds chicken pieces (drumsticks, thighs, cut-up*
> *breasts)*
> *3 cloves garlic, crushed*
> *2 teaspoons anchovy paste*
> *1 tablespoon chili powder*
> *1 tablespoon ground coriander*
> *1 tablespoon ground turmeric*
> *1½ teaspoons minced fresh ginger*
> *4 tablespoons salad oil*
> *1 large onion, peeled and chopped*
> *1½ cups coconut milk*
> *1 tablespoon brown sugar*
> *Juice of 1 lime*
> *3 medium-sized potatoes, peeled and cut into 1½-inch*
> *cubes*

Remove skin from chicken pieces and wipe dry with paper toweling. Mash garlic, anchovy paste, chili powder, coriander, turmeric, ginger, and 1 tablespoon oil in a small bowl. Sauté onion in 3 tablespoons heated oil in a large deep skillet until tender. Add spice mixture; fry 2 minutes. Add chicken pieces and fry on all sides to coat well with spice mixture and until any redness disappears. Add remaining ingredients and cook slowly, uncovered, about 45 minutes, until chicken and potatoes are tender. Turn chicken pieces with tongs a few times while cooking. Serves 6.

South African Lamb-Fruit Curry

This is an innovative curry that can be served for a dinner or made in larger quantity for a buffet.

12 dried apricots
½ cup seedless raisins
1 cup hot water
2 pounds boneless lamb shoulder, cut into small cubes
3 tablespoons salad oil
1 large onion, peeled and chopped
2 tablespoons curry powder
¼ teaspoon cayenne pepper
3 tablespoons vinegar
1 tablespoon sugar
1 large tart apple, peeled, cored, and diced
2 medium-sized carrots, scraped and diced
2 tablespoons apricot jam
2 tablespoons shredded coconut
Garnishes: 2 bananas, sliced; 1 green pepper, cleaned
  and chopped; 1 large tomato, peeled and chopped

Put apricots and raisins into a small bowl. Cover with water and let soak 1 hour. Wipe lamb cubes dry and brown on all sides in heated oil in a large saucepan. Remove to a plate. Sauté onion in drippings until tender. Add curry powder, cayenne, vinegar, and sugar. Cook 2 minutes. Return lamb to saucepan. Add apricots, raisins, and water. Bring to a boil. Lower heat and cook slowly, covered, 1 hour. Add apple and carrots. Continue cooking about 45 minutes longer, until ingredients are tender. Add a little more water during cooking, if needed. Mix in jam and coconut 5 minutes before cooking is finished. Serve on a platter topped with garnishes. Serves 6.

Bengal Fish Curry

In the East Indian region of Bengal seafood is available in abundance and is used to make superb curries flavored with hot spices, yogurt, and mustard oil. Serve for a weekend brunch.

> 2 pounds fish (cod, halibut, flounder) fillets, cut into 1-
>   inch cubes
> 1 tablespoon ground turmeric
> 1 teaspoon ground red pepper
> ½ teaspoon ground ginger
> Salt, pepper to taste
> 3 tablespoons mustard or salad oil
> 2 medium-sized onions, peeled and sliced
> 2 cloves garlic, crushed
> 2 bay leaves
> 6 cardamom seeds, crushed
> 1 teaspoon mustard seeds
> 1 1-inch cinnamon stick
> 2 large tomatoes, peeled and chopped
> 1 cup plain yogurt

Rub fish cubes with turmeric, red pepper, ginger, salt, and pepper. Fry in heated oil on all sides in a large deep skillet. Remove fish to a plate. Add onions and garlic to drippings and sauté until tender. Push aside. Add bay leaves, cardamom and mustard seeds, and cinnamon; fry 1 or 2 minutes. Add tomatoes and yogurt and cook slowly, uncovered, 5 minutes. Add fish and cook slowly, covered, 10 minutes. Remove and discard bay leaves and cinnamon stick. Serves 4.

Georgia Country Captain

This version of chicken curry was introduced to Georgia by British settlers. It is a good main dish for an outdoor luncheon.

> *1 broiler-fryer chicken, about 2½ pounds, cut up*
> *2 to 3 tablespoons curry powder*
> *1 teaspoon paprika*
> *1½ teaspoons salt*
> *½ teaspoon pepper*
> *3 tablespoons salad oil*
> *1 large onion, peeled and chopped*
> *2 cloves garlic, crushed*
> *1 large green pepper, cleaned and chopped*
> *1 can (1 pound) tomatoes, chopped*
> *½ teaspoon dried thyme*
> *3 cups hot cooked rice*
> *½ cup currants or chopped seedless raisins*
> *⅓ cup slivered blanched almonds*

Remove skin from chicken pieces and pat dry with paper toweling. Sprinkle outer surfaces with curry powder, paprika, salt, and pepper. Rub gently with fingers to press spices and salt into chicken. Fry in heated oil on all sides in a large deep skillet until golden. Remove to a plate with tongs. Add onion and garlic to drippings; sauté until tender. Add green pepper, tomatoes, and thyme. Cook slowly, uncovered, 10 minutes. Return chicken pieces to skillet and cook slowly, covered, about 30 minutes, until chicken is tender. Turn once or twice during cooking. Serve chicken pieces over hot rice on a platter. Top with sauce and sprinkle with currants or raisins and almonds. Serves 4.

South Seas Fish Curry

This is an easy to prepare curry for an informal supper.

> 1½ pounds white-fleshed fish fillets (cod, flounder,
>   halibut), cut into 1½-inch cubes
> 2 to 3 tablespoons curry powder
> 3 tablespoons peanut or salad oil
> 2 large onions, peeled and chopped
> 2 to 3 cloves garlic, crushed
> 1 teaspoon minced fresh ginger
> 2 large tomatoes, peeled and chopped
> Juice of 1 lime or lemon
> 1 teaspoon salt
> ¼ teaspoon pepper
> ⅓ cup chopped fresh coriander or parsley

Pat fish cubes dry with paper toweling. Sprinkle with curry powder. Fry in heated oil on all sides in a large deep skillet for 5 minutes. Remove to a plate. Add onions and garlic to drippings; sauté until tender. Add ginger, tomatoes, lime or lemon juice, salt, and pepper. Cook, stirring, 5 minutes. Add fish cubes and cook slowly, covered, about 15 minutes, until tender. Add a little more water during cooking, if needed. Mix in coriander or parsley just before serving. Serves 4.

South African Babotie

This curry flavored ground meat dish makes a colorful luncheon entrée.

1 slice white bread
1 cup milk
1 pound ground beef or lamb
2 eggs
1 large tart apple, peeled, cored, and minced
⅓ cup chopped seedless raisins
1 medium-sized onion, peeled and chopped
1 tablespoon butter or margarine
1 to 2 tablespoons curry powder
2 teaspoons sugar
1 teaspoon salt
¼ teaspoon pepper
2 tablespoons fresh lemon juice
12 blanched almond slivers

Put bread in a small bowl. Cover with milk. Let soak until soft. Squeeze bread dry. Reserve drained milk. Put bread in a large bowl. Add beef or lamb, 1 egg, apple, and raisins; mix well. Sauté onion in heated butter or margarine in a small skillet until tender. Add curry powder, sugar, salt, pepper, and lemon juice. Cook 1 minute. Add to meat mixture; mix well. Spoon into a 10-inch pie plate or shallow baking dish. Smooth top with a spatula, flattening it evenly. Dot with almonds. Combine reserved milk and remaining egg; beat with a wire whisk. Slowly pour over meat mixture. Bake in a preheated 350° oven 45 minutes, until meat is cooked and custard is set. Serves 4.

Madras Shrimp Curry

This is an elegant curry to serve for a late evening supper.

2 pounds uncooked shelled and deveined shrimp
1 medium-sized onion, peeled and minced
2 cloves garlic, crushed
2 teaspoons ground turmeric
1 teaspoon ground coriander
1 teaspoon minced fresh ginger
½ teaspoon ground cumin
Salt, pepper to taste
3 tablespoons clarified butter or salad oil
1 cup coconut milk
1 tablespoon fresh lime juice
¼ cup chopped fresh coriander or parsley

Wash shrimp and pat dry with paper toweling. Whirl onion, garlic, turmeric, coriander, ginger, cumin, salt, and pepper in a blender, or mash. Fry mixture in heated butter or oil in a large deep skillet for 2 minutes. Add shrimp and cook gently, turning once or twice, about 10 minutes, until shrimp begin to turn pink. Add coconut milk and simmer, uncovered, 5 minutes. Remove shrimp to a serving dish and keep warm. Reduce sauce until thickened. Add lime juice. Pour sauce over shrimp. Serve garnished with coriander or parsley. Serves 4 to 6.

Australian Meat-Fruit Curry

Australians prepare this steamed version of curry with leftover cooked beef, lamb, chicken, or turkey. Sometimes additional fruits such as chopped mangos, melons, or papayas are added.

The curry is a good entree for a summer luncheon.

> 2 medium-sized onions, peeled and chopped
> 2 tablespoons peanut or salad oil
> 2 to 3 tablespoons curry powder
> 4 cups diced cooked meat or poultry
> 2 large tart apples, peeled, cored, and diced
> 3 bananas, peeled and diced
> 2 tablespoons chopped chutney
> 1 cup seedless raisins
> ½ cup diced dates
> 2 tablespoons brown sugar
> 1 cup water

Sauté onions in heated oil in a large saucepan until tender. Add curry powder and cook 1 minute. Add remaining ingredients. Do not mix. Cook slowly, covered, 1 hour. Add a little more water during cooking, if needed. Serve garnished with lemon wedges and chopped parsley, if desired. Serves 6.

Goa Pork Vindaloo

In Western India sharp and tasty curries called *vindaloos* are flavored with vinegar, spices, and mustard oil. They are generally made with duck, fish, shrimp, or pork. This version is a good supper entrée.

> 1 large onion, peeled and quartered
> 4 cloves garlic
> 1 teaspoon mustard seeds
> 1 1-inch piece ginger, minced
> 4 whole cloves

1 teaspoon cumin seeds
1 teaspoon ground red pepper
2 teaspoons salt
¾ cup vinegar
2 tablespoons mustard or salad oil
2 pounds boneless pork, cut into 1½-inch cubes
2 medium-sized tomatoes, peeled and cubed
3 medium-sized potatoes, peeled and cubed
2 teaspoons sugar

Put first eight ingredients in a blender; add 2 tablespoons vinegar; blend a few seconds. Fry ground mixture in heated oil in a deep skillet 2 minutes. Wipe pork cubes dry and brown on all sides in oil. Add remaining vinegar and cook slowly, covered, 1 hour. Add tomatoes, potatoes, and sugar and continue cooking about 30 minutes longer, until pork and potatoes are tender. Serves 6.

English Kedgeree

This favorite English breakfast dish originated in India, where it was made with a variety of leftover cooked foods such as lentils, rice, and eggs. Adapted and popularized by the English, it has been customarily prepared by them with smoked or cooked fish, rice, hard-cooked eggs, and various seasonings, including curry powder. This is one of the many versions. It is an easy to prepare entrée for a weekend brunch.

2 to 3 tablespoons curry powder, preferably Madras
⅓ cup butter or margarine
2 tablespoons fresh lemon juice
2½ cups cooked rice

2½ *cups flaked cooked fish (cod, salmon, haddock, or*
    tuna)
1 *tablespoon Worcestershire sauce*
4 *hard-cooked eggs, shelled and chopped*
½ *cup chopped fresh parsley*
Salt, pepper to taste

Fry curry powder in heated butter or margarine 2 minutes in a large saucepan. Add lemon juice, rice, and fish. Cook slowly, stirring, until foods are heated. Mix in remaining ingredients and leave on medium heat long enough to heat through and blend flavors. Serves 6.

Burmese Shrimp-Bamboo Shoot Curry

This is an interesting curry for a Sunday luncheon.

2 *large onions, peeled and sliced*
2 *tablespoons salad oil*
1 *tablespoon ground turmeric*
1 *teaspoon ground red pepper*
1 *tablespoon water*
2 *teaspoons minced fresh ginger*
2 *cloves garlic, crushed*
2 *pounds uncooked shelled and deveined shrimp*
1 *cup coconut milk*
½ *cup sliced bamboo shoots, drained*
⅓ *cup chopped fresh coriander or parsley*
⅓ *cup chopped almonds*

Fry onions in heated oil in a large deep skillet until tender. Add turmeric, red pepper, and water. Cook slowly, uncovered, 2 minutes. Add ginger and garlic; cook 1 minute. Add shrimp, coconut milk, and bamboo shoots. Cook slowly, covered, about 10 minutes, until shrimp turn pink and are just tender. Serve garnished with coriander or parsley and almonds. Serves 4.

Thai Red Beef Curry

You will enjoy this curry, made with flank steak, white onions, and green pepper, for a small dinner.

1 flank steak, about 1¼ pounds
1 cup coconut milk
1 can (4 ounces) red curry sauce
2 teaspoons brown sugar
3 tablespoons fish or soy sauce
2 tablespoons fresh lemon juice
12 small white onions, peeled and cooked
1 large green pepper, cleaned and cut into strips

Remove any fat and membrane from steak. Cut across the grain into small strips, about 2½″ × ½″. Skim heavy cream from top of coconut milk and heat 1 minute in a large deep skillet. Add curry sauce and cook 2 minutes. Add meat strips and stir to coat well with sauce. Add remaining coconut milk, sugar, fish sauce, and lemon juice. Cook slowly, uncovered, stirring occasionally, 10 minutes, until beef is cooked and sauce is reduced slightly. Add onions and green pepper 2 minutes before cooking is finished. Serves 4.

Ceylonese Meatball Curry

The southeast Asian island of Ceylon, now called Sri Lanka, has many kinds of regional curries that differ in color and seasonings but are generally quite hot. This specialty is a good entrée for a Sunday night supper.

> *2 pounds ground beef or lamb*
> *3 cloves garlic, crushed*
> *¼ cup minced onions*
> *1 tablespoon chili powder*
> *1 tablespoon ground coriander*
> *½ teaspoon ground cumin*
> *1½ teaspoons salt*
> *½ teaspoon pepper*
> *2 tablespoons* garam masala *(or ground spice mixture)*
> *3 tablespoons peanut or salad oil*
> *1 cup coconut milk*
> *1 1-inch piece stick cinnamon*
> *2 bay leaves*
> *Juice of 1 lime or lemon*

Combine beef or lamb with garlic, onions, chili powder, coriander, cumin, salt, and pepper in a large bowl. Shape into 2-inch balls. Cook *garam masala* in heated oil in a large skillet 2 minutes. Add meatballs, several at a time, and brown on all sides. Add remaining ingredients and cook slowly, uncovered, about 30 minutes, until meatballs are cooked. Remove and discard cinnamon stick and bay leaves. Serves 6.

North Indian Lamb Korma

Curries called *kormas* are made with meat cubes which are marinated and cooked in a spicy yogurt mixture. This is a good entrée for a company dinner.

> *2 pounds boneless lamb, cut into 1½-inch cubes*

1 cup plain yogurt
1 tablespoon ground turmeric
½ teaspoon ground cumin
1½ teaspoons salt
½ teaspoon pepper
2 tablespoons poppy seeds
¼ cup shredded coconut
½ cup blanched almond slivers
3 cloves garlic, crushed
1 teaspoon ground red pepper
½ teaspoon ground ginger
2 large onions, peeled and minced
3 tablespoons peanut or salad oil
½ teaspoon each ground cinnamon, cloves, and nutmeg
3 tablespoons chopped fresh coriander or mint leaves
3 tablespoons fresh lime or lemon juice

Combine lamb, yogurt, turmeric, cumin, salt, and pepper in a large saucepan. Leave to marinate 1 hour. Cook slowly, covered, 1 hour. Grind or pound poppy seeds, coconut, almonds, garlic, red pepper, and ginger. Sauté onions in heated oil in a small skillet. Add ground mixture; cook 2 minutes. Add to partially cooked lamb mixture and continue cooking 30 minutes longer, until lamb is tender. Stir in coriander or mint leaves and lime or lemon juice 5 minutes before cooking is finished. Serves 4 to 6.

Jamaican Curried Lamb

On the Caribbean island of Jamaica a traditional curry is prepared with goat or kid. Lamb is a good substitute. Serve for a weekend luncheon or dinner.

3 pounds boneless shoulder or leg of lamb, cut into 1½-inch cubes

3 to 4 tablespoons salad oil
2 large onions, peeled and chopped
3 to 4 tablespoons curry powder, preferably Madras
1 teaspoon ground hot peppers
1 teaspoon ground allspice
1 bay leaf
2 teaspoons salt
· ½ teaspoon pepper
1 cup beef bouillon
2 large tomatoes, peeled and chopped
1 cup coconut milk
2 tablespoons fresh lime or lemon juice

Wipe lamb cubes dry. Brown in heated oil on all sides in a large deep skillet. Remove to a plate. Add onions to drippings and sauté until tender. Mix in curry powder, peppers, allspice, bay leaf, and salt. Cook 2 minutes. Return lamb to skillet. Add bouillon and bring to a boil. Cook slowly, covered, 1 hour. Add tomatoes, coconut milk, and lime or lemon juice and continue cooking, uncovered, 45 minutes longer, until lamb is tender. Serves 6 to 8.

Indian Tandoori Chicken

Tandoori chicken is a popular Indian home and restaurant specialty that originated in a northwest region which is now a part of Pakistan. The name derives from a clay oven called *tandoor* in which various foods are cooked. The flavorful chicken is marinated in yogurt and spices before cooking. You can cook the chicken on an outdoor grill over hot charcoal or in a kitchen oven. Serve for a summer luncheon or dinner.

1 medium-sized onion, peeled and quartered
4 cloves garlic, chopped

2 teaspoons chopped fresh ginger
1 teaspoon ground red pepper
2 teaspoons ground turmeric
½ teaspoon each ground cinnamon, cloves, and nutmeg
2 teaspoons garam masala
3 tablespoons fresh lemon juice
1½ cups plain yogurt
6 chicken legs
6 chicken thighs
Garnishes: 1 lemon, sliced; 1 onion, sliced and separated
into rings; 1 cup fresh coriander or mint leaves

Combine onion, garlic, spices, *garam masala*, lemon juice, and yogurt in a blender container; whirl several seconds until smooth. Turn into a large bowl or shallow dish. Remove skin from chicken and make several slashes in flesh of each piece. Add to yogurt-spice mixture. Leave to marinate 24 hours or longer, turning a few times. Arrange chicken pieces in a roasting pan. Brush with marinade. Cook in a preheated 400° oven 25 minutes, until chicken is tender and slightly charred. Turn once or twice during cooking. Serves 6.

Pakistan Beef Biryani

A curry dish called *biryani* is made in Pakistan and India with cubes of meat first cooked with yogurt and spices and then baked with rice. It is a good dish for a dinner party.

1 large onion, peeled and chopped
2 cloves garlic, crushed
2 tablespoons salad oil
1 teaspoon minced fresh ginger
6 whole cloves
8 cardamom seeds, crushed

2 1-inch pieces stick cinnamon
1 teaspoon ground coriander
2 teaspoons ground turmeric
1½ pounds boneless beef, cut into 1-inch cubes
1 cup plain yogurt
3 cups water
1½ cups uncooked long grain rice
1½ teaspoons salt
½ teaspoon pepper
⅛ teaspoon saffron
½ cup milk

Sauté onion and garlic in heated oil in a large deep skillet until tender. Add ginger, 3 cloves, 4 cardamom seeds, 1 stick cinnamon, coriander, and turmeric. Cook 2 minutes. Add beef and yogurt. Cook slowly, covered, 1 hour. Meanwhile, bring water to a boil in a medium-sized saucepan. Add rice, remaining 3 cloves, 4 cardamom seeds, 1 stick cinnamon, salt, and pepper. Reduce heat and cook slowly, covered, about 12 minutes, until rice is partially cooked and most of liquid has been absorbed. When meat is cooked, remove and discard cloves and cinnamon. Spoon beef and rice in alternate layers into a 3-quart casserole, topping with a layer of rice. Mix saffron with milk and pour over rice. Bake, tightly covered, in a preheated 350° oven 45 minutes. Serves 4.

Note: Sprinkle top with melted butter or margarine and paprika if saffron is not used.

Thai Chicken Curry

This appealing curry is a good dish for a weekend luncheon.

2 chicken breasts, 1 pound each
1 tablespoon ground coriander
1 tablespoon chili powder
4 teaspoons ground turmeric
1 teaspoon ground cumin
½ teaspoon pepper
1 tablespoon anchovy paste
1 medium-sized onion, peeled and minced
4 cloves garlic, crushed
1½ cups coconut milk
Juice of 1 lemon
3 tablespoons fish sauce
2 tablespoons dried basil

Skin and bone chicken; cut into small strips about ½"×3". Grind coriander, chili powder, turmeric, cumin, pepper, anchovy paste, onion, and garlic in a blender or mortar. Skim heavy cream from top of coconut milk and cook 1 minute in a large deep skillet. Add ground spice-onion mixture and ½ cup coconut milk; cook 5 minutes. Add chicken strips and stir to coat all sides with mixture. Add remaining coconut milk, lemon juice, and fish sauce. Cook slowly, uncovered, 15 minutes, stirring occasionally. Mix in basil just before serving. Serves 4 to 6.

Indian Chicken Masalam

Tomato purée and yogurt add a pleasing flavor to this traditional curry. Serve for a weekend dinner.

3 pounds chicken pieces, thighs, drumsticks, cut-up
   breasts
2 large onions, peeled and sliced
2 cloves garlic, crushed

3 tablespoons salad oil
2 bay leaves
1 tablespoon ground coriander
2 teaspoons ground turmeric
2 teaspoons chili powder
½ teaspoon ground cumin
½ cup tomato purée
½ cup plain yogurt
¼ cup water
1 tablespoon garam masala

Remove skin from chicken pieces and wipe dry with paper toweling. Sauté onions and garlic in heated oil in a large deep skillet until tender. Add spices and cook 2 minutes. Add chicken pieces and fry on all sides to coat well with spices and until any redness disappears. Add tomato purée, yogurt, and water. Cook slowly, covered, about 40 minutes, until chicken is tender. Add *garam masala* 5 minutes before cooking is finished. Serves 6.

American Curried Veal

This is a good curry for a buffet.

2 large onions, peeled and sliced
2 cloves garlic, crushed
3 tablespoons salad oil
2 to 3 tablespoons curry powder
2 pounds veal shoulder, cut into 1-inch cubes
2 tablespoons all-purpose flour
1 teaspoon salt
¼ teaspoon pepper
½ cup tomato juice
1 cup beef bouillon

*Condiments: Peanuts, chutney, chopped bananas,
crumbled fried bacon, grated coconut, chopped raisins*

Sauté onions and garlic in heated oil in a deep large skillet until tender. Add curry powder and cook 1 or 2 minutes. Dust veal cubes with flour seasoned with salt and pepper. Push onions aside and brown veal cubes on all sides in drippings. Add tomato juice and bouillon. Bring to a boil. Reduce heat and cook slowly, covered, 1½ hours, until veal is tender. Serve over rice accompanied by condiments. Serves 6 to 8.

Pot Roasts
and Hot Pots

One-dish meals cooked in pots are old-fashioned favorites that have particular appeal today since they are made with relatively inexpensive meats or poultry and are cooked slowly to enhance flavor and tenderness.

Pot roasts and hot pots lend themselves to experimentation because one can prepare them in great variety. You can alter the old-time specialties with foods of your choice to serve for family or company meals. The dishes are hearty and nourishing, and, while particularly suitable in cold weather, they are good at any time of the year.

Although any kind of meat or poultry can be pot roasted, less tender cuts of meat that would be too tough or dry if roasted are generally used. The long, slow cooking process breaks down the fibers of the meat and tenderizes it. Pot roasts are made with large pieces of meat or whole poultry that are sliced or cut up at the time of serving.

Beef cuts are most popular for pot roasting. You may use them in one piece with or without bones, or deboned and rolled. Particularly suitable are all cuts of beef chuck, brisket, rump, bottom round, flank, eye of the round, or sirloin tip. Pork shoulder, tenderloin, butt or arm roast; lamb shoulder, leg, or breast; veal shoulder, breast, or rump; variety meats; whole chickens, ducklings, or small turkeys are appropriate, too.

Traditionally the method of preparing a pot roast is to brown the meat evenly on all sides in hot fat or oil in an uncovered pot on top of the stove. Browning should be done slowly over moderate heat to keep the meat from drying on the outside and to brown it more thoroughly. When turning the meat use two wooden or metal spoons. Never pierce the meat with a fork or other sharp implement. Flouring the meat before cooking enhances the flavor and richness of the gravy and drippings.

When the meat has been browned, put it on a rack in the pot to keep the underside from getting too brown. Add a small amount of liquid. More can be added during cooking, if needed. Then add any seasonings and cover tightly. Simmer gently on top of the stove or in a slow oven, if you wish. Cooking at a high temperature shrinks the meat and makes the fibers tough. Vegetables and/or other foods can be added when the meat is partially cooked. The liquid can be used to make gravy after cooking, if desired.

Cook long enough to reach the well-done stage. Exactly how long, will depend on the size and quality of the food. Beef chuck for example, requires considerably more time than chicken.

One of the versatile features of pot roasts is that you can make a given piece of meat into an entirely different dish by varying the liquid, changing various seasonings, and adding vegetables or other foods. Some roasts are enhanced by marinating in a flavorful liquid before cooking.

Any number of different utensils can be used for cooking pot roasts. The Dutch oven, pot or kettle should be large enough to hold the foods and it should be made of good heavy-gauge material. A tight-fitting lid will keep the liquid from boiling away and it will hold in the steam needed to make the meat tender.

Although often regarded as everyday family fare, pot roasts have much to recommend them for party entrées. They may be cooked ahead of time, they wait beautifully, and they will serve a number of persons. Remember also that leftover pot roast is excellent fare.

Unlike pot roasts, hot pots are made with cut-up meats and vegetables which are cooked slowly for a long time in the oven or on top of the stove. Oriental hot pots, also called fire pots, differ in that the utensil is a stovelike round metal dïsh with a circular basin in which foods are dipped and cooked in a hot broth or other liquid.

European hot pots date back to the thirteenth century when French cooks prepared them as a kind of ragout to which bread or breadcrumbs were added as thickeners. The dish was called a *hochepot,* a name derived from the word for mixture and also for an earthenware pot in which it was cooked.

Hot pots in varying forms became favorite winter fare in several northern European countries, where they are still served as national dishes. The Dutch call the dish *hutspot.* In England it is known simply as hot potch. Scots use the words hotch potch.

Hot pots are flavorful mixtures that are sometimes topped with mashed potatoes or pastry. They are cooked in colorful oven-proof dishes or casseroles that usually can be brought to the table.

You will enjoy serving hot pots for family meals or small informal suppers. They can be prepared beforehand and are made with inexpensive but interesting ingredients.

The following recipes for pot roasts and hot pots are representative of those enjoyed in the past and today in Europe and America.

Basic Pot Roast

This is a basic beef pot roast that can be prepared with herbs according to taste and may include one or more vegetables ranging from celery to turnips. It is superb for a family meal.

1 3½- to 4-pound boneless beef pot roast
3 tablespoons all-purpose flour
2 teaspoons salt
½ teaspoon pepper
3 tablespoons shortening or salad oil
1 cup water, beef bouillon or other liquid
1 bay leaf
¾ teaspoon dried thyme, basil, marjoram, or oregano
2 sprigs parsley

Wipe beef dry. Rub on all sides with flour seasoned with salt and pepper. Brown on all sides in heated shortening or oil in a heavy kettle. Put a rack in kettle under beef. Add remaining ingredients. Bring to a boil. Lower heat and cook slowly, covered, about 3 hours, until meat is tender. Remove and discard bay leaf and parsley. Slice beef and serve with sauce. Serves 6 to 8.

Note: Add 3 large carrots, sliced; 6 medium-sized potatoes, peeled; and 6 medium-sized onions, peeled; 50 minutes before cooking is finished, if desired.

Beef A La Mode

The French classic, *Boeuf à la Mode,* beef braised in red wine with vegetables, is one of the finest dishes in the world. It is a well-seasoned pot roast that in France is cooked with calve's feet to give flavor and to add body to the stock. The dish may be served hot, garnished with its vegetables, or it may be served cold with a jellied sauce. This is a handsome dish to serve for a company dinner or buffet.

1 4- to 4½-pound boneless beef pot roast
2 tablespoons salad oil
1 cup dry red wine
1 bay leaf
4 whole cloves
½ teaspoon dried thyme
3 sprigs parsley
2 teaspoons salt
½ teaspoon pepper
8 small carrots, scraped
16 small white onions, peeled
8 small potatoes, peeled
1 tablespoon all-purpose flour (optional)

Wipe beef dry. Brown on all sides in heated oil in a heavy kettle. Put a rack in kettle under beef. Add wine, bay leaf, cloves, thyme, parsley, salt, and pepper. Bring to a boil. Lower heat and cook slowly, covered, about 3½ hours, until meat is tender. Add vegetables 50 minutes before cooking is finished. Slice beef and serve with vegetables and sauce. Thicken sauce with flour, if desired. Serves 8.

Yankee Pot Roast

This old time New England beef and vegetable dish sometimes

includes salt pork and parsnips as well as the ingredients in this recipe. One version also called for raisins. It is a good company or family supper dish. Serve with warm corn bread.

1 3½- to 4-pound boneless beef pot roast
3 tablespoons all-purpose flour
2 teaspoons salt
½ teaspoon pepper
3 tablespoons bacon drippings or shortening
1 cup beef bouillon or water
1 bay leaf
4 sprigs parsley
6 medium-sized onions, peeled
6 small carrots, scraped
6 medium-sized potatoes, peeled
2 small white turnips, peeled and cubed

Wipe beef dry. Rub on all sides with flour, seasoned with salt and pepper. Brown on all sides in heated drippings or shortening in a heavy kettle. Put a rack into kettle under beef. Add water, bay leaf, and parsley. Cook slowly, covered, 2 hours. Add vegetables and cook about 50 minutes longer, until meat is tender and vegetables are cooked. Slice beef and serve with vegetables and sauce. Serves 6 to 8.

Mexican Pork Roast with Vegetables

An attractive and delicious pot roast for a company Saturday night dinner. Serve with warm corn muffins or bread.

1 large onion, peeled and sliced
2 cloves garlic, crushed
2 tablespoons olive or salad oil

1 4-pound boned and rolled pork loin
2 to 3 teaspoons chili powder
2 teaspoons salt
½ teaspoon pepper
1 can (1 pound) tomatoes, chopped
1 can (8 ounces) tomato sauce
1 teaspoon dried oregano
1 can (12 ounces) whole kernel corn, drained
1 package (10 ounces) frozen cut-up green beans
3 tablespoons chopped fresh coriander or parsley

Sauté onion and garlic in heated oil in a heavy kettle until tender. Push aside and add pork loin that has been rubbed with chili powder, salt, and pepper. Brown on all sides in drippings. Spoon off any fat. Add tomatoes, tomato sauce, and oregano. Add remaining ingredients during last 15 minutes of cooking. Slice pork and serve with vegetables and sauce. Serves 6 to 8.

Swedish Royal Pot Roast

This piquant flavored pot roast called *slottsstek* is served surrounded with small mounds of cooked vegetables such as potatoes, peas, carrots, or cauliflower. Red currant jelly is a traditional accompaniment.

1 3½- to 4-pound boneless beef pot roast
2 teaspoons salt
¼ teaspoon pepper
3 tablespoons butter or margarine
¾ cup beef bouillon
2 medium-sized onions, peeled and sliced
3 flat anchovy fillets, drained and minced
1 bay leaf

1 teaspoon ground allspice
2 tablespoons white vinegar
2 tablespoons all-purpose flour
½ cup heavy cream
3 cups seasoned hot green peas
3 cups seasoned hot diced carrots

Rub beef with salt and pepper. Brown on all sides in heated butter or margarine in a heavy kettle. Put a rack in kettle under beef. Add bouillon, onions, anchovies, bay leaf, allspice, and vinegar. Cook slowly, covered, about 3 hours, until beef is tender. Slice beef; keep warm. Strain liquid. Scrape pan drippings, add flour and mix well. Add some of strained liquid and the cream. Cook slowly, stirring, until thickened and smooth. Pour a little gravy over meat slices; serve remaining gravy separately. Surround with green peas and carrots. Serves 6 to 8.

Pennsylvania Dutch Sweet-Sour Pot Roast with Noodles

This is a well-flavored hearty dish to serve for a family dinner.

1 3½- to 4-pound boneless beef pot roast
2 cups cider
2 tablespoons brown sugar
¼ teaspoon ground cinnamon
⅛ teaspoon ground cloves
¼ cup all-purpose flour
2 teaspoons salt
½ teaspoon pepper
3 tablespoons butter or margarine
1 large onion, peeled and sliced

1 can (6 ounces) tomato paste
2 large carrots, scraped and sliced
1 package (8 ounces) egg noodles, cooked and drained

Put beef into an earthenware crock or non-aluminum deep container. Cover with cider, sugar, cinnamon, and cloves. Leave in refrigerator, covered, 24 hours. Take beef from marinade and pat dry with paper toweling. Strain and reserve marinade. Brown beef on all sides in heated butter or margarine in a heavy kettle. Put a rack in kettle under beef. Add 1 cup reserved marinade, onion, and tomato paste; mix well. Cook slowly, covered, 2 hours, adding more marinade, if necessary. Add carrots and cook about 50 minutes longer, until meat is tender and carrots are cooked. Mix in cooked noodles. Slice beef and serve with noodles, vegetables, and sauce. Serves 6 to 8.

Italian Veal Pot Roast with Mushrooms

A superb pot roast to serve for a weekend dinner.

1 4-pound boneless rolled veal shoulder
3 tablespoons all-purpose flour
2 teaspoons salt
½ teaspoon pepper
2 tablespoons butter or margarine
2 tablespoons olive oil
1 large onion, peeled and sliced
2 cloves garlic, crushed
2 medium-sized carrots, scraped and chopped
2 stalks celery, diced
2 bay leaves
1 teaspoon dried thyme

1 cup dry white wine
¾ pound medium-sized fresh mushrooms, cleaned

Wipe veal dry. Rub on all sides with flour, seasoned with salt and pepper. Brown on all sides in heated butter or margarine and oil in a heavy kettle. Remove to a platter. Sauté onion, garlic, carrots, and celery in drippings 5 minutes. Top with a rack. Place browned veal on rack. Add bay leaves, thyme, and wine. Cook slowly, covered, about 3 hours, until veal is tender. Add mushrooms during last 15 minutes of cooking. Remove veal to a warm platter; slice. Serve with vegetables and sauce. Serves 6 to 8.

Cape Cod Cranberry Pot Roast

Early settlers in Massachusetts discovered that the tart cranberry was an appealing and versatile addition to many dishes, including pot roasts. This is a good fall or winter holiday entrée.

1 3½- to 4-pound boneless beef pot roast
3 tablespoons all-purpose flour
2 teaspoons salt
½ teaspoon pepper
3 tablespoons shortening or salad oil
½ cup water
2 cups strained cooked cranberry sauce
4 whole cloves
½ inch cinnamon stick

Wipe beef dry. Rub on all sides with flour, seasoned with salt and pepper. Brown on all sides in heated shortening or oil in a heavy kettle. Put a rack in kettle under beef. Add remaining ingredients and cook slowly, covered, about 3 hours, until beef is tender. Slice beef and keep warm. Strain sauce and pour over beef. Serves 6 to 8.

Israeli Beef Cholent

This traditional meal-in-one-dish is of Central European origin and has long been prepared for Sabbath meals. Because cooking on the Sabbath is forbidden, the dish is prepared ahead of time. The name is believed to have derived from the French word *chaud,* warm. It is a good supper dish.

½ pound dried lima beans
2 medium-sized onions, peeled and sliced
2 large carrots, scraped and sliced
3 tablespoons chicken fat or shortening
½ cup pearl barley
8 medium-sized potatoes, pared
3½- to 4-pound corned beef brisket
3 tablespoons brown sugar
¼ teaspoon pepper

Soak beans in water to cover overnight or for 8 hours. Sauté onions and carrots in heated fat or shortening in a large kettle for 5 minutes. Drain beans and add, with barley and potatoes, to kettle. Push ingredients aside and place beef brisket in center of them. Cover with water and add sugar and pepper. Cook very slowly, covered tightly, on top of stove about 3 hours, until beef is tender, adding additional water if necessary. Shake kettle occasionally to prevent ingredients from sticking to the bottom. Slice beef thin across the grain and keep warm. Surround with vegetables and cover with sauce. Serves 6.

Minnesota Venison Pot Roast

This inviting pot roast can be made with venison, if available, or beef. Serve for a winter dinner.

> 1 4½- to 5-pound venison shoulder roast
> 1 clove garlic, halved
> 2 cups dry red wine or water
> 2 slices lemon
> 1 large onion, peeled and sliced
> 1 bay leaf
> 2 sprigs parsley
> 2 teaspoons salt
> ½ teaspoon pepper
> 3 tablespoons bacon fat or shortening
> 1 cup sour cream

Put venison into an earthenware crock or nonaluminum deep container. Cover with remaining ingredients, except fat and sour cream. Leave in refrigerator, covered, 1 to 2 days. Turn venison once or twice. Take from marinade and pat dry with paper toweling. Strain and reserve marinade. Brown venison on all sides in heated fat in a heavy kettle. Put a rack in kettle under venison. Add reserved marinade. Cook slowly, covered, about 3 hours, until venison is tender. Slice venison and keep warm. Scrape drippings, add sour cream, and heat slowly. Pour over venison. Serves 8.

Danish Fruit-Stuffed Pork Tenderloin

This interesting pot-roasted pork specialty is a good company dinner entrée.

2 pork tenderloins, about 1 pound each
12 prunes, scalded and pitted
2 large tart apples, cored, peeled, and chopped
Salt, pepper to taste
2 tablespoons butter or margarine
1 cup water
2 tablespoons all-purpose flour
1 cup heavy cream

Remove any membranes from pork and slit each tenderloin lengthwise two-thirds through to form a pocket. Fill each pocket with prunes and apples seasoned with salt and pepper. Tie with string to keep stuffing inside pockets. Brown each tenderloin on all sides in heated butter or margarine in a heavy kettle. Add water and cook slowly, covered, 1 hour. Check during cooking to see if more water is needed. Remove pork to warm platter, slice, and keep warm. Skim any fat from sauce and scrape drippings. Mix in flour; cook 1 minute. Add cream and heat slowly. Serve over pork. Serves 4.

New England Boiled Dinner

This well-known early American one-dish meal was traditional fare in the homes of our forefathers. The trick in preparation is to have all the ingredients finish cooking at the same time. The beets, however, are cooked separately and served with the corned beef and other vegetables. A good dish for a family winter dinner.

1 3½- to 4-pound corned beef brisket
6 medium-sized potatoes, peeled
6 medium-sized carrots, scraped
6 medium-sized white turnips, peeled and quartered

1 medium-sized green cabbage, cored and quartered
6 medium-sized beets, washed
Salt, pepper to taste

Wipe corned beef with damp paper toweling. Place into a large kettle. Cover with cold water. Bring to a boil. Reduce heat and simmer 5 minutes. Skim surface. Simmer, covered, 3½ to 4 hours, until beef is tender, adding additional water if necessary. About 45 minutes before cooking is finished, skim fat from surface. Add potatoes, carrots, and turnips. Add cabbage 20 minutes before cooking is finished. Meanwhile, cook beets separately in salted boiling water for 35 minutes, until tender. Slip off skins and keep warm. Slice beef thin across the grain. Place in center of a large warm platter. Surround with vegetables and cover with sauce. Season with salt and pepper, if desired. Serves 6 to 8.

French Pot-Roasted Chicken

In France a whole chicken which is browned in a flameproof casserole in butter or other fat, covered with a flavorful sauce, and cooked on top of the stove or in the oven until tender, is called *poulet en cocotte*. Serve for a weekend luncheon.

1 roasting chicken, 3½ to 4 pounds
Salt, pepper to taste
4 sprigs fresh tarragon or 2 teaspoons dried tarragon
3 tablespoons butter or margarine
2 tablespoons olive or salad oil
16 small white onions, peeled
½ cup tomato sauce
1 bouquet garni (1 bay leaf, ½ teaspoon dried thyme, 2
sprigs parsley, wrapped in cheesecloth)

16 small white potatoes, peeled
1 pound fresh mushrooms, cleaned
1 package (9 ounces) frozen artichoke hearts

Wash chicken and pat dry with paper toweling. Season inside and out with salt and pepper. Put tarragon in chicken's cavity. Truss chicken with heavy thread. Brown chicken on all sides in heated butter and oil in a heavy casserole, turning carefully with two spoons so skin is not torn. Remove to a platter or pan. Add onions to drippings; sauté 5 minutes. Stir in tomato sauce. Add *bouquet garni.* Put chicken on a rack in kettle. Cover tightly and cook on top of stove about 1 hour, until chicken is tender. Add potatoes after chicken has been cooking 30 minutes. Add mushrooms and artichokes after cooking 45 minutes. Remove chicken from casserole and cut up. Serve with vegetables and cover with sauce. Serves 4.

German Sauerbraten

This well-known German pot roast is cooked in a wine marinade and flavored with gingersnap crumbs. Small dumplings or boiled potatoes can be added to the dish, if desired. A good dish for a late evening winter supper.

1 4½- to 5-pound boneless beef pot roast
1 cup dry red wine
1 cup red wine vinegar
1 cup cold water
1 large onion, peeled and sliced thin
2 bay leaves
8 peppercorns, bruised
4 whole cloves
4 sprigs parsley

Salt
3 tablespoons all-purpose flour
½ teaspoon pepper
3 tablespoons shortening or salad oil
1 cup diced onion
1 large carrot, scraped and diced
8 gingersnaps, crumbled

Put beef into an earthenware crock or nonaluminum deep container. Combine wine, vinegar, water, onion, bay leaves, peppercorns, cloves, parsley, and 2 teaspoons salt in a saucepan. Bring to a boil. Pour over beef and cool. Leave in refrigerator, covered, 24 hours. Take meat from marinade and pat dry with paper toweling. Strain marinade and reserve. Rub meat with flour, seasoned with salt and pepper. Brown meat on all sides in heated shortening or oil in a heavy kettle. Remove to a platter with two large spoons. Add onion and carrot to drippings; sauté 5 minutes. Add 3 cups reserved marinade and bring to a boil. Return meat to kettle. Simmer, covered, 2½ hours, until meat is tender. Take meat from kettle and put on a warm platter. Bring remaining liquid to a boil. Add gingersnaps. Cook 1 or 2 minutes until thickened. Remove from heat. Slice beef and cover with sauce. Serves 8 to 10.

French Lamb Pot Roast with Beans

A hearty pot roast for a weekend luncheon.

1 3½- to 4-pound boned and rolled lamb shoulder roast
1 teaspoon dried rosemary, crumbled
1 teaspoon dried thyme
2 teaspoons salt

½ *teaspoon pepper*
2 *tablespoons olive or salad oil*
2 *medium-sized onions, peeled and sliced*
2 *cloves garlic, crushed*
2 *tablespoons fat or salad oil*
2 *large tomatoes, peeled and chopped*
1 *cup dry white wine*
3 *cups cooked or canned white beans, drained*
3 *tablespoons chopped fresh parsley*

Rub lamb with rosemary, thyme, salt, and pepper. Brown on all sides in heated oil in a heavy kettle. Remove lamb and pour off all fat except 1 tablespoon. Sauté onion and garlic in heated fat until tender. Put lamb on a rack in the kettle. Add tomatoes and wine. Cook slowly, covered, about 2½ hours, until lamb is tender. Add beans and parsley 10 minutes before cooking is finished. Slice lamb and serve with beans and sauce. Serves 6 to 8.

Hungarian Pot Roast Esterházy

This pot-roasted steak is cooked with vegetables, flavored with sour cream, and garnished with lemon slices and capers. It is an excellent entrée for a company dinner.

3 *pounds boneless beef chuck or round steak*
2 *teaspoons salt*
½ *teaspoon pepper*
2 *tablespoons butter or margarine*
2 *medium-sized turnips, peeled and cut in strips*
2 *medium-sized onions, peeled and chopped*
2 *medium-sized carrots, scraped and sliced*
2 *stalks celery, sliced*

1 bay leaf
½ teaspoon dried thyme
1 cup beef bouillon
2 tablespoons all-purpose flour
1 cup sour cream, at room temperature
½ lemon, sliced
1 tablespoon capers, drained

Rub beef with salt and pepper. Brown on all sides in heated butter or margarine in a heavy kettle. Remove to a plate. Sauté vegetables in butter drippings 5 minutes. Return beef to kettle and put a rack under it. Add bay leaf, thyme, and bouillon. Cook slowly, covered, about 2½ hours, until beef is tender. Slice beef and keep warm. Blend flour with sour cream. Gradually add to gravy, stirring as adding, and cook over low heat until thickened and smooth. Spoon sauce over beef. Garnish with lemon slices and capers. Serves 6.

Belgian Wine-Flavored Pot Roast

This beef pot roast is cooked in a wine marinade and includes mushrooms. Serve for a company dinner.

1 3½- to 4-pound boneless beef pot roast
2 cups dry red wine
1 large onion, peeled and sliced
1 large carrot, scraped and sliced
1 bay leaf
3 whole cloves
2 sprigs parsley
2 teaspoons salt
½ teaspoon pepper
3 tablespoons butter or margarine

2 tablespoons all-purpose flour
1 tablespoon Worcestershire sauce
¾ pound fresh mushrooms, thick sliced
3 tablespoons chopped fresh parsley

Put beef into an earthenware crock or nonaluminum deep container. Cover with wine, onion, carrot, bay leaf, cloves, parsley sprigs, salt, and pepper. Leave in refrigerator, covered, 24 hours. Take out beef and pat dry with paper toweling. Strain and reserve marinade. Brown on all sides in heated butter or margarine in a heavy kettle. Put a rack in kettle under beef. Add reserved marinade. Cook slowly, covered, about 2¾ hours, until beef is tender. Slice beef and keep warm. Add flour to sauce; cook slowly, stirring, until thickened and smooth. Add Worcestershire sauce and mushrooms; cook slowly 3 minutes. Spoon over beef slices. Sprinkle with parsley. Serves 6 to 8.

Spanish Pot-Roasted Duckling

This is an innovative dish for a weekend luncheon.

1 duckling, 4 to 5 pounds
1 tablespoon olive oil
2 large onions, peeled and sliced
2 large green peppers, cleaned and chopped
1 can (8 ounces) tomato sauce
½ cup dry red or white wine
1½ teaspoons salt
¼ teaspoon pepper
12 large pitted green olives
2 tablespoons chopped fresh parsley
3 cups hot cooked long grain rice

Wash duckling and pat dry. Brown in heated oil in a heavy kettle. Pour off all fat except 2 tablespoons. Add onions and green peppers; sauté 2 minutes. Put duckling on a rack in kettle. Add tomato sauce, wine, salt, and pepper. Cook slowly, covered, 1½ hours, until duckling is tender. Stir in olives and parsley. Cut up duckling; serve over rice; cover with sauce. Serves 4.

Polish Hussar's Roast

This Polish version of a pot roast can be blanched with vodka instead of vinegar, if desired. It is a good company dinner entrée.

4 pounds boneless beef, rump or round
½ cup hot vinegar
3 tablespoons all-purpose flour
2 teaspoons salt
½ teaspoon pepper
5 tablespoons butter or margarine
½ cup hot beef bouillon
1 large onion, peeled and sliced
1 cup fresh bread cubes
1 large onion, peeled and grated or minced
1 egg, slightly beaten

Scald beef with hot vinegar; wipe dry with paper toweling. Sprinkle beef with flour, seasoned with salt and pepper. Brown beef on all sides in 3 tablespoons heated butter or margarine in a large kettle. Add bouillon and sliced onion. Cook very slowly, tightly covered, 2 hours. Turn twice while cooking. Meanwhile, combine bread cubes, grated or minced onion, egg, and remaining 2 tablespoons butter, melted. Season with salt and pepper, if desired. Take beef from kettle. Cut from top to about one inch from bottom into ¼" slices so slices are apart but not separate.

Place stuffing between slices. Skewer meat at each end; bind roast with heavy thread. Carefully return to kettle. Sprinkle with a little flour and baste with drippings. Cook slowly, covered, 30 minutes, until beef is tender. Remove to a warm platter. Remove thread and skewers. Slice beef. Thicken liquid with a little flour to use as a gravy, if desired. Serves 8.

Dutch Hodgepodge

This traditional Dutch dish, called *hutspot,* is served annually on October 3rd to celebrate the end of the Spanish seizure of Leyden in 1574, when it was used to feed the starving populace. This is a good entree for a late evening supper.

1 flank steak, about 2 pounds
2 teaspoons salt
4 cups water
6 medium-sized carrots, scraped and sliced
2 large onions, peeled and chopped
6 medium-sized potatoes, peeled and quartered
3 tablespoons light cream or milk
3 tablespoons butter or margarine
½ teaspoon pepper

Cut any membranes and fat from flank steak. Put into a large saucepan with 1 teaspoon salt and water. Bring to a boil. Lower heat and simmer, covered, 1 hour. Add carrots, onions, and potatoes; simmer another 45 minutes, until steak and vegetables are cooked. Slice beef thin across the grain; keep warm. Mash vegetables with cream, butter, 1 teaspoon salt, and pepper. Thin with a little hot liquid, if desired. Spoon vegetables onto center of a large warm platter. Surround with steak strips. Serves 4.

German Beef-Vegetable Hot Pot

Sweet-and-sour flavored beef short ribs are cooked with vegetables in this hot pot from Germany. It is a good dish for a family dinner.

> *3 pounds beef short ribs, cut into 3-inch pieces*
> *¼ cup all-purpose flour*
> *2 teaspoons salt*
> *½ teaspoon pepper*
> *2 tablespoons shortening or salad oil*
> *2 tablespoons wine vinegar*
> *2 tablespoons brown sugar*
> *1½ cups beef bouillon or water*
> *½ small rutabaga, peeled and cubed*
> *2 large carrots, scraped and sliced*
> *2 large onions, peeled and quartered*

Dredge beef ribs with flour, seasoned with salt and pepper. Brown on all sides in heated shortening or oil in a heavy kettle. Add vinegar, sugar, bouillon or water. Bake, covered, in a preheated 300° oven 2½ hours, until beef is tender. Add vegetables after cooking 1 hour. Serve ribs surrounded with vegetables and covered with sauce. Serves 4.

Irish Corned Beef and Cabbage

This hearty dinner-in-a-pot has long been favorite fare in Ireland and America. Peeled whole potatoes can be added to the dish during the last 25 minutes of cooking, if desired. This is a good entrée for a weekend supper.

1 4½- to 5-pound corned beef brisket
1 medium-sized onion stuck with 4 cloves
1 large onion, peeled and sliced
1 large carrot, scraped and sliced
½ teaspoon dried thyme
2 bay leaves
6 peppercorns
1 medium-sized green cabbage, cored and cut in wedges

Wipe corned beef with damp paper toweling. Place into a large kettle. Cover with cold water. Bring to a boil. Reduce heat and simmer 5 minutes. Skim surface. Add remaining ingredients, except cabbage. Simmer, covered, 3½ to 4 hours, until beef is tender. Add cabbage during last 20 minutes of cooking. Slice beef thin across the grain. Place in center of a large warm platter. Surround with vegetables. Serves 8 to 10.

Lancashire Hot Pot

This lamb-potato dish originated in Northern England's county of Lancashire, where it was prepared for the daily evening meal. Serve for a family supper.

2 pounds neck of lamb, sliced
3 tablespoons lard or margarine
1 large onion, peeled and sliced
½ pound fresh mushrooms, cleaned and sliced
    lengthwise
3 lamb kidneys, sliced
6 shucked oysters (optional)
6 medium-sized potatoes, peeled and sliced thick
1 cup beef bouillon

2 teaspoons sugar
Pinch mace or nutmeg
1½ teaspoons salt
¼ teaspoon pepper

Brown lamb slices on all sides in heated lard or margarine in a large skillet. Remove to an ovenproof casserole. Add onions to drippings and sauté until tender. Spoon over lamb. Put mushrooms, kidneys, and oysters in layers over onions. Arrange potato slices, overlapping each other, to cover the top. Combine remaining ingredients and pour over casserole ingredients. Bake, covered, in a preheated 350° oven about 2 hours, until ingredients are cooked. Remove cover during last 30 minutes of cooking so top will become golden. Serve lamb and kidneys surrounded with vegetables and covered with sauce. Serves 6.

Scottish Hotch Potch

In Scotland this hearty lamb-vegetable pot, also called harvest broth, is traditionally made with neck of lamb and several fresh vegetables in season. This is a variation of the dish. Serve for a family supper.

3 pounds neck or breast of lamb, cut up
1½ teaspoons salt
½ teaspoon pepper
1 cup chicken broth or water
2 large carrots, scraped and sliced
2 large onions, peeled and quartered
2 cups shelled green peas
6 scallions, cleaned and sliced
1 teaspoon sugar
1 tablespoon chopped fresh mint

Brown lamb on all sides in a heavy kettle. Pour off fat. Season with salt and pepper. Add chicken broth or water and simmer, covered, 1½ hours. Add carrots and onions and continue cooking 30 minutes longer. Add remaining ingredients and cook about 20 minutes longer, until lamb and vegetables are cooked. Serves 4.

Casseroles

Americans have become extremely fond of casseroles in recent years. Small wonder, for there are noteworthy advantages in preparing and serving these excellent culinary creations. Prized for their versatility and convenience, they can be prepared with an almost limitless choice of ingredients and they are truly international.

Casserole cookery dates to prehistory when early cooks combined foods in utensils of clay or brick pottery. The term casserole, however, originated in France much later, probably in the early 1700s. It developed from *casse*, the name for a large and deep round utensil in which many ingredients were cooked slowly for a long time.

Through the centuries the cooks of many lands created marvelous culinary combinations which were slowly simmered or baked in various types of utensils. These became widely known as casseroles.

The early colonists and later immigrants from all corners of the globe introduced many of their national casseroles to the New World. Necessity often demanded that local ingredients be utilized. Thus new creations or adaptations of old favorites were developed in America. Many an early church supper, neighborhood get-together, family reunion, or holiday outing featured a one-pot casserole or an array of what became known as "covered dish" meals.

During the nineteenth century, as America's wealth increased and gastronomic elegance demanded elaborate meals of many courses, casseroles were relegated to the status of ordinary fare. But after World War II, when harried homemakers were forced to manage kitchens and homes without help and sought out easier and more inventive ways of preparing and serving meals, casserole cookery regained prominence. Seemingly everyone began to create and savor casseroles.

Over the years the word "casserole" acquired a double meaning in America. It is used for the utensil itself, but it has also become synonymous with a one-dish meal cooked in a bake-and-serve dish. While a casserole may be cooked either on top of the stove or in the oven, the selection in this book includes only those that are baked.

Casseroles are prepared with just about every kind of meat, poultry, and seafood, with succulent combinations of pastas, cereals, vegetables, and other foods. They may be plain or fancy, light or hearty, simply seasoned or highly spiced. Some are mere combinations of canned and/or frozen foods which are quickly mixed and cooked. Others are elaborate mixtures of numerous ingredients, and perhaps intricate sauces, that require considerable preparation and longer cooking. Even homely baked dishes such as hashes or dough-covered foods are served as casseroles.

Casserole cookery is flexible. In choosing the foods, however, only top quality ingredients should be used. While some dishes call for leftover cooked meats, poultry, and/or vegetables, fresh foods are generally preferable. The best selections are those which marry well and complement each other in texture, flavor, and color. Generally, casseroles are made with cut-up or bite-size foods that are firm and easy to serve and eat. Some mixtures are entirely precooked; others consist of some precooked ingredients together with others that will cook rapidly.

An important aspect of making casseroles is the proper amount of liquid or sauce to assure a moist but not overly fluid dish. Various foods differ in the amounts of liquid they'll absorb. Casseroles made with pasta or rice, for example, require more liquid than those made with potatoes or vegetables, such as mushrooms, which secrete liquid. A covered casserole will contain moisture; an uncovered dish will not.

Casserole ingredients should be carefully seasoned so that flavorings blend well with the primary ingredients. Generally speaking, it is wise to limit the choice of spices or herbs to one or two and be sure that they complement the other foods. Toppings, such as buttered bread crumbs, mashed potatoes, or cheese combinations add extra touches and give an attractive appearance to many casseroles.

Most casseroles should be cooked at a moderate temperature of 350° or 375° so that the ingredients blend well and heat slowly. High heat toughens the food and detracts from its flavor, nutrients and tenderness. If liquid has to be added to a casserole while cooking, it should first be heated; never add cold liquid to hot food.

Today we are indeed fortunate in having available as utensils beautifully fashioned casserole dishes of infinite variety. Casseroles can be cooked in virtually any kind of heatproof container, round, square, oval or oblong; and small, medium, or large. It may be any color of the rainbow and made of glazed pottery, heat-proof glass, earthenware, and enamelled cast iron, aluminum, or stainless steel. Besides a wide American-made selection, you may choose from imported products. Most have a lid and two handles.

When cooking in casseroles remember that sudden changes in temperature should be avoided. Don't put cold ingredients into a hot casserole; don't place an empty casserole on heat; and don't pick one up with a cloth or pot holder that is wet. When serving, place the casserole on a hot pad, trivet, or heat resistant surface.

Most casseroles can be easily frozen, if desired. They should not, however, include foods that do not freeze well, such as hard-cooked egg whites, mayonnaise or sauces that might separate, boiled potatoes, salad greens or other raw vegetables. You can prepare and mix all the ingredients and freeze the casserole uncooked. Or, you can prepare and bake the casserole and then freeze it.

Freeze a cooked casserole as soon as possible after it has been thoroughly cooled. Wrap completely and tightly. It may remain frozen from two to six months depending on the ingredients. Before serving, the casserole may be thawed in the refrigerator and baked 30 minutes, or put into the oven while still frozen and baked 1 to 1½ hours. Either way, reheat at a moderate temperature.

While casseroles are excellent for any occasion, they are perfect for informal meals served at the table or buffet style. They may be enjoyed either indoors or out using casual colorful appointments. The dishes can be made in advance and cooked when you like. Brought to the table hot and bubbly from the oven, casseroles require less work at that stage because they can easily be served from the dishes in which they are cooked.

This selection of casseroles is designed to display the versatility and cosmopolitan appeal of an inviting category of one-dish meals. You will enjoy them either for the family or company entertaining.

Greek Beef-Macaroni Casserole

This favorite Greek casserole called *pastitsio* is an excellent entrée for an outdoor meal.

> *1 large onion, peeled and chopped*
> *2 tablespoons salad oil*
> *1½ pounds lean ground beef*
> *1 cup dry red wine*
> *1 can (6 ounces) tomato paste*
> *1 teaspoon ground cinnamon*
> *1½ teaspoons salt*
> *½ teaspoon pepper*
> *¼ cup butter or margarine*
> *¼ cup all-purpose flour*
> *2 cups milk*
> *⅛ teaspoon grated nutmeg*
> *3 egg yolks*
> *3 cups elbow macaroni*
> *2 eggs*
> *About ¾ cup fine dry bread crumbs*
> *½ cup grated Parmesan cheese*

Sauté onion in heated oil in a large skillet until tender. Add beef and cook, separating with a fork, until redness disappears. Add wine, tomato paste, cinnamon, salt, and pepper. Cook briskly, uncovered, 5 minutes. Remove from heat. Melt butter or margarine in a saucepan; stir in flour and cook slowly 1 minute. Gradually add milk, stirring as adding, and cook about 10 minutes, until smooth and thickened. Season with nutmeg and salt and pepper, if desired. Mix a spoonful or two of hot white sauce into egg yolks; return to sauce. Cook, stirring, 1 minute longer. Remove from heat. Cook macaroni according to package directions until tender; drain. Add eggs and mix well. To assemble casserole, sprinkle a well-buttered 2½-quart shallow baking dish with bread crumbs. Spoon half cooked macaroni mixture into dish, spreading evenly. Cover with meat sauce and sprinkle with ¼ cup grated cheese. Cover with remaining macaroni and then white sauce. Sprinkle top with remaining ¼ cup grated cheese. Bake in preheated 350° oven, uncovered, 1 hour, until ingredients are cooked, sauce is set, and top is lightly golden. Cut in squares. Serves 6.

Italian Eggplant Parmigiana

This popular eggplant specialty derives its name from Parmesan cheese, *parmigiano*. Serve for a luncheon.

> *2 medium-sized eggplants, about 1¼ pounds each,*
> *   washed and stemmed*
> *Salt*
> *About 1 cup olive or salad oil*
> *1 large onion, peeled and chopped*
> *1 can (6 ounces) tomato paste*
> *2¼ cups water*
> *1 teaspoon dried basil*
> *½ teaspoon dried oregano*
> *¼ teaspoon pepper*
> *About 1 cup all-purpose flour*
> *2 to 3 eggs, beaten*
> *¾ pound mozzarella cheese, sliced*
> *1 cup grated Parmesan cheese*

Cut eggplants crosswise into slices about ¼" thick. Put into a colander; sprinkle with salt. Leave to drain 30 minutes. Wipe dry with paper toweling. Sauté onions in 2 tablespoons heated oil in a large skillet until tender. Mix in tomato paste, water, basil, oregano, 1 teaspoon salt, and pepper. Cook slowly, uncovered, 20 minutes, stirring occasionally. Remove from heat. Dust each eggplant slice with flour; dip in beaten egg. Fry on both sides in hot oil in another skillet until soft and golden, adding more oil as needed. Drain on paper toweling. Line a shallow baking dish, about 2½ quarts, with a little of the tomato sauce. Arrange a layer of eggplant slices over it. Cover with a layer of mozzarella slices, more sauce, and a sprinkling of grated cheese. Repeat layers to use all ingredients. Bake in preheated 350° oven 30 minutes, until tender and golden on top. Serves 6.

California Beef-Spaghetti-Zucchini Casserole

This is a colorful easy-to-prepare casserole for a buffet.

1 medium-sized onion, peeled and chopped
2 cloves garlic, crushed
2 tablespoons salad oil
2 pounds lean ground beef
1 can (10½ ounces) tomato purée
1 can (6 ounces) tomato paste
1½ cups water
4 flat anchovy fillets, drained and minced
1 tablespoon capers, drained
¼ cup chopped fresh parsley
¾ teaspoon salt
¼ teaspoon pepper
1 pound spaghetti
2 tablespoons butter or margarine
2 cans (1 pound each) zucchini with tomato sauce
About ⅓ cup grated Parmesan cheese

Sauté onion and garlic in heated oil in a large skillet until tender. Add beef and cook, separating with a fork, until redness disappears. Add tomato purée, tomato paste, water, anchovies, capers, parsley, salt, and pepper; mix well. Cook slowly, uncovered, 30 minutes. Meanwhile, cook spaghetti in boiling water until just tender; drain. Spoon into a large bowl. Add butter or margarine and toss with two forks to mix well. When beef mixture is cooked, spoon half the spaghetti, half the zucchini, and half the cheese into a 3½- to 4-quart shallow baking dish. Top with half the beef mixture. Repeat the layers, topping with grated cheese. Cook in a preheated 375° oven 30 minutes, until cooked and golden on top. Serves 12.

Danish Meatball-Noodle Casserole

This attractive casserole is a good entrée for a family dinner.

1 medium-sized onion, peeled and minced
5 tablespoons butter or margarine
1 cup soft bread crumbs
½ cup milk
2 pounds ground beef or mixture of beef, pork and veal
1 egg, beaten
½ teaspoon allspice
1½ teaspoons salt
½ teaspoon pepper
3 tablespoons all-purpose flour
2 cups beef bouillon
1 package (12 ounces) egg noodles, cooked and drained
1 teaspoon caraway seeds
2 jars or 2 cans (1 pound each) sweet-sour red cabbage
2 tablespoons chopped fresh dill or parsley

Sauté onion in 1 tablespoon heated butter or margarine in a small skillet until tender. Spoon into a large bowl. Soak bread crumbs in milk until soft; add to onion. Add beef, egg, allspice, salt, and pepper; combine well. Shape into 2-inch balls. Brown in 2 tablespoons heated butter or margarine on all sides in an extra large skillet. Sprinkle with flour and mix. Gradually add bouillon, stirring as adding, and cook slowly, covered, 30 minutes, until meatballs are cooked. Spoon into a 3-quart shallow baking dish, reserving liquid. Top with red cabbage, spreading evenly. Combine warm cooked noodles with remaining 2 tablespoons butter or margarine and caraway seeds. Spoon over cabbage, spreading evenly. Pour liquid from meatballs over ingredients. Sprinkle top with dill or parsley. Bake in preheated 350° oven 30 minutes. Serves 8.

Provençal Baked Eggs and Vegetables

This is an attractive brunch or luncheon entrée.

1 medium-sized eggplant, about 1¼ pounds
About 1 cup olive or salad oil
2 cloves garlic, crushed
2 medium-sized onions, peeled and chopped
4 medium-sized tomatoes, peeled and chopped
1 teaspoon dried oregano
1½ teaspoons salt
¼ teaspoon pepper
8 eggs
½ cup chopped fresh parsley

Cut off eggplant stem. Wash and cut eggplant into 1-inch cubes. Wipe dry. Fry cubes, several at a time, in heated oil in a large skillet until tender and golden. Remove to a plate as cooked.

Add garlic and onions to drippings; sauté until tender. Add tomatoes, oregano, salt, and pepper; mix well and cook 5 minutes. Spoon eggplant cubes into center of a round shallow baking dish. Surround with onion-tomato mixture. Make 8 depressions with back of a large spoon in vegetables. Break an egg into each depression. Sprinkle top with parsley. Bake in a preheated 350° oven about 12 minutes, until eggs are set. Serves 4.

Mexican Vegetable-Filled Enchiladas

This is a good casserole for a brunch or supper.

2 cans (8 ounces each) tomato sauce
2 cloves garlic, crushed
1 teaspoon dried oregano
3 to 4 teaspoons chili powder
1½ teaspoons salt
½ teaspoon pepper
16 prepared or canned tortillas
About ⅔ cup salad oil
2 cups drained, cooked or canned corn
2 cups drained, cooked or canned pinto or red beans
2 medium-sized onions, peeled and chopped
1½ cups grated Monterey Jack or Cheddar cheese

Combine tomato sauce, garlic, oregano, chili powder, salt, and pepper in a small saucepan. Bring to a boil. Reduce heat and cook slowly, uncovered, 10 minutes. Fry tortillas, one at a time, on both sides in heated oil in a skillet until limp. Spoon one heaping tablespoon of corn and one of beans along center of each tortilla. Sprinkle with chopped onions and roll up around filling. Arrange, seam sides down, next to each other in a greased shallow baking dish. Top with tomato sauce and sprinkle with grated cheese. Bake in a preheated 350° oven 30 minutes, until ingredients are hot and cheese is melted. Serves 4.

English Toad in the Hole

This easy-to-prepare baked sausage specialty is a good brunch dish.

1 cup all-purpose flour
1 cup milk
2 eggs, beaten
1 teaspoon salt
¼ teaspoon pepper
1 pound pork sausages or slices of cooked beef

Combine flour, milk, eggs, salt, and pepper in a large bowl; mix well to form a thick batter. Leave 30 minutes. If sausages are to be used, cook and drain them. Place sausages or beef in a shallow baking dish; cover with batter, spreading evenly. Bake in preheated 400° oven 30 minutes, until crust is cooked and flaky. Serves 4.

Rumanian Pork-Sauerkraut Casserole

This is a hearty casserole for a winter dinner.

1 large onion, peeled and sliced
2 leeks, white parts only, cleaned and sliced
3 tablespoons shortening or salad oil
2 pounds sauerkraut, drained
2 tablespoons all-purpose flour

¼ cup tomato paste
2 cups beef bouillon
1 teaspoon sugar
1 tablespoon fresh lemon juice
2 tablespoons chopped fresh dill or parsley
Salt to taste
½ teaspoon pepper
2 pounds smoked pork or ham, cut into 2-inch cubes

Sauté onion and leeks in heated shortening or oil in a medium sized skillet until tender. Remove to a large bowl; add sauerkraut and mix well. Set aside. Stir flour into drippings; mix well. Add tomato paste, bouillon, sugar, lemon juice, dill or parsley, salt, and pepper. Cook slowly, uncovered, 5 minutes. Arrange pork or ham and sauerkraut mixture in layers in a shallow baking dish. Top with tomato sauce. Bake in a preheated 325° oven 1 hour. Serve with sour cream, if desired. Serves 6 to 8.

Greek Fish-Vegetable Casserole

This baked specialty called *plaki* can be served hot or cold. It is a good entrée for a summer luncheon.

2 pounds white-fleshed fish fillets (flounder, cod, halibut)
Salt, pepper to taste
2 large onions, peeled and sliced
3 medium-sized leeks, white parts only, washed and
*   sliced (optional)*
2 cloves garlic, crushed
⅓ to ½ cup olive or salad oil
3 large tomatoes, peeled and sliced
3 medium-sized carrots, scraped and sliced thin
1 cup sliced celery

2 bay leaves
1 teaspoon dried oregano
2 medium-sized lemons, sliced
⅓ cup chopped fresh parsley

Wash fish and sprinkle on all sides with salt and pepper. Set aside. Sauté onions, leeks, and garlic in heated oil in a medium sized skillet until tender. Add tomatoes, carrots, celery, bay leaves, and oregano; sauté 5 minutes. Spoon into a shallow baking dish, spreading evenly. Arrange fish fillets over vegetable mixture. Top with lemon slices. Bake in a preheated 350° oven about 30 minutes, until fish is just tender. Sprinkle with parsley 5 minutes before cooking is finished. Serves 4 to 6.

Continental Turkey-Mushroom Hash

This is a wine and cream flavored hash. Serve for a brunch or luncheon.

1 large onion, peeled and chopped
1 medium-sized green pepper, peeled and minced
About ¼ cup butter or margarine
2 tablespoons all-purpose flour
1 cup light cream
½ cup dry white wine
1½ teaspoons salt
½ teaspoon pepper
4 cups diced cooked turkey or chicken
½ pound sliced fresh mushrooms, previously sautéed in
  butter
⅓ cup fine dry bread crumbs
⅓ cup grated Parmesan cheese

Sauté onion and green pepper in 3 tablespoons heated butter or margarine in a large saucepan until tender. Stir in flour; blend well. Add cream, stirring, until thickened and smooth. Add wine, salt and pepper. Cook, stirring, 1 or 2 minutes. Mix in turkey or chicken and mushrooms. Cook 1 minute. Spoon into a buttered shallow baking dish. Sprinkle with bread crumbs and cheese. Dot with butter. Bake in a preheated 400° oven about 20 minutes, until hot and bubbly. Serves 4.

Southwestern Beef-Cornmeal Casserole

This well-known casserole called tamale pie is a hearty dish for a winter supper.

1 large onion, peeled and chopped
2 cloves garlic, crushed
2 tablespoons salad oil
2 tablespoons chili powder
1 pound lean ground beef
½ cup minced green pepper
1 can (1 pound) tomatoes, chopped
1 can (6 ounces) tomato paste
1 teaspoon dried oregano
2½ teaspoons salt
½ teaspoon pepper
3 cups water
1 cup yellow cornmeal
6 pitted black olives, halved
½ cup grated Jack or Cheddar cheese

Sauté onion and garlic in heated oil in a large skillet until tender. Add chili powder and cook 1 minute. Add beef and cook, mixing with a fork, until redness disappears. Mix in green pepper, tomatoes with liquid, tomato paste, oregano, 1½ teaspoons salt, and pepper. Cook slowly, uncovered, 20 minutes. Meanwhile, put water and remaining 1 teaspoon salt in a large saucepan; bring to a boil. Slowly add cornmeal, stirring as adding with a wooden spoon. Reduce heat and cook about 20 minutes, stirring frequently, until thickened. Line a 1½-quart shallow baking dish with half the cooked cornmeal. Top with meat mixture, spreading evenly. Top with remaining cornmeal, spreading evenly. Decorate top with olives. Bake in a preheated 350° oven 45 minutes. Sprinkle with cheese 15 minutes before cooking is finished. Serves 6.

Near Eastern Lamb-Stuffed Squash

These flavorful lamb and rice stuffed squash are served with a yogurt sauce. Serve for luncheon or supper.

1 small onion, peeled and minced
2 tablespoons salad oil
1 pound ground lamb
¾ cup cooked long grain rice
¼ cup chopped pine nuts or almonds
¾ teaspoon ground cinnamon
¼ teaspoon ground nutmeg
1½ teaspoons salt
½ teaspoon pepper
6 medium-sized tender yellow squash, washed and
 stemmed
2 tablespoons all-purpose flour
2 cups plain yogurt at room temperature
¼ cup chopped fresh mint or parsley

Sauté onion in heated oil in a medium sized skillet until tender. Add lamb and cook, stirring, until redness disappears. Pour off any fat. Add rice, nuts, spices, and salt. Mix well and remove from heat. Cut each squash in half lengthwise. Scoop out pulp to form shells, discarding it or reserving to cook later, leaving an even ¼-inch thick border. Spoon lamb-rice mixture into squash shells, heaping into a mound at the top. Arrange in an extra large shallow baking dish. Add water, ½-inch deep. Cook, covered with foil, in a preheated 375° oven 45 minutes. Remove from oven and take out squash: put onto a plate and keep warm. Spoon 2 tablespoons liquid from baking dish into a small saucepan; stir in flour. Add yogurt and leave on stove long enough to heat through. Stir in mint or parsley. Serve with squash. Serves 6.

Yugoslavian Meat-Vegetable Casserole

This Yugoslavian national dish is called *djuvec* and is made with varying ingredients according to regional tastes. Potatoes, for example, can be used instead of rice. It is a good entrée for a family dinner.

> 4 medium-sized onions, peeled and sliced
> ½ cup olive or salad oil
> 2 pounds lean boneless pork, cut into 1½-inch cubes
> 1 pound boneless lamb, cut into 1½-inch cubes
> 1½ teaspoons salt
> ½ teaspoon pepper
> 4 large tomatoes, peeled and sliced
> 1 medium-sized eggplant, about 1½ pounds, stemmed
>   and cubed
> 2 small zucchini, stemmed and sliced
> 4 medium-sized green peppers, cleaned and cubed

1 cup cut-up green beans
1 cup uncooked long grain rice

Sauté onions in heated oil in a large skillet until tender. Push aside. Wipe pork and lamb cubes dry; brown on all sides in oil. Add salt and pepper. Remove from heat. Arrange onions, meat, vegetables, and rice in layers in a large shallow baking dish, topping with a layer of tomato slices. Add enough water to barely cover ingredients. Bake, covered, in a preheated 350° oven 1½ hours, until ingredients are tender. Uncover during last 30 minutes of cooking. Serves 8.

American Chicken-Sausage-Bean Casserole

This hearty casserole is a good entrée for a winter dinner.

1 pound dried Great Northern beans, washed and picked
   over
6 cups water
1 cup chopped celery
1 cup scraped chopped carrots
3 chicken bouillon cubes
1 fryer-broiler chicken, about 2½ pounds, cut up
3 tablespoons salad oil
1 smoked sausage, about 1 pound, cut into 1-inch pieces
1 large onion, peeled and chopped
2 cloves garlic, chopped
1 can (15 ounces) tomato sauce
½ teaspoon dried oregano
2 teaspoons salt
½ teaspoon pepper
⅓ cup chopped fresh parsley

Put beans and water into a large kettle. Bring to a boil; boil 2 minutes. Remove from heat and let stand, covered, 1 hour. Add celery, carrots, and bouillon cubes. Bring to a boil again. Lower heat and cook slowly, covered, until beans are tender, about 1 hour. Meanwhile, wipe chicken pieces dry. Fry in heated oil in a large skillet until golden on all sides. Remove to a heavy 3-quart casserole. Add sausage slices to drippings and fry. Remove to the casserole. Add onion and garlic to drippings; sauté until tender. Add tomato sauce, oregano, salt, and pepper. Cook slowly, uncovered, 10 minutes. When beans are tender, drain, reserving liquid. Spoon beans, carrots, and celery over chicken and sausages. Add 1 cup bean liquid and tomato sauce. Bake, covered, in a preheated 325° oven 1 hour, until ingredients are tender. Sprinkle with parsley 10 minutes before cooking is finished. Serves 6.

Turkish Eggplant Moussaka

This well-known casserole is a good entrée for an informal luncheon or supper.

> 2 medium-sized onions, peeled and chopped
> 2 cloves garlic, crushed
> About 1 cup olive or salad oil
> 1 pound lean ground beef
> 2 tablespoons tomato paste
> ½ teaspoon dried oregano
> ¼ cup chopped fresh parsley
> 1½ teaspoons salt
> ½ teaspoon pepper
> ½ cup water
> 2 medium-sized eggplants, about 1¼ pounds each,
>   washed

¼ cup butter or margarine
¼ cup all-purpose flour
2 cups hot milk
2 eggs, beaten
½ cup grated Parmesan cheese
Pinch grated nutmeg

Sauté onions and garlic in 2 tablespoons heated oil in a large skillet until tender. Add beef and cook, separating with a fork, until redness disappears. Add tomato paste, oregano, parsley, salt, pepper, and water. Cook, uncovered, 20 minutes. Meanwhile, cut unpeeled eggplant into thin lengthwise slices. Fry in heated oil, a few slices at a time, until tender and golden on both sides, adding more oil as needed. Arrange alternate layers of eggplant and beef mixture in a 2-quart shallow baking dish, beginning and ending with a layer of eggplant. Melt butter or margarine in a small saucepan; stir in flour and cook 1 minute. Gradually add milk, stirring as adding. Cook slowly, stirring, until thickened and smooth. Spoon some of mixture to mix with eggs. Return to sauce. Add cheese and nutmeg. Mix well. Spoon into baking dish to cover top layer of eggplant. Bake in preheated 350° oven 30 minutes, until mixture is set and golden on top. Cool slightly before serving. Serves 6.

Texas Sausage-Chick-Pea Casserole

This is a good casserole for a luncheon or supper.

1 pound bulk sausage
1 large onion, peeled and minced
2 cloves garlic, crushed
1 large green pepper, cleaned and diced
1 can (8 ounces) tomato sauce

2 to 3 teaspoons chili powder
½ teaspoon ground cumin
1½ teaspoons salt
¼ teaspoon pepper
1 can (1 pound, 4 ounces) chick-peas, drained
½ cup sliced black olives
3 tablespoons chopped fresh parsley
1 cup shredded Jack or Cheddar cheese

Cook sausage in a medium sized skillet, stirring with a fork, until redness disappears. Remove to a plate. Add onion, garlic, and green pepper to drippings; sauté until tender. Add tomato sauce, chili powder, cumin, salt, and pepper; cook slowly, uncovered, 10 minutes. Combine with sausage and chick-peas in a shallow baking dish. Top with olives and parsley. Sprinkle with shredded cheese. Bake in a preheated 350° oven, uncovered, 30 minutes. Serves 4.

Egyptian Chicken Liver-Rice Casserole

Serve this casserole for a brunch or luncheon.

6 tablespoons butter or margarine
3 cups chicken broth
1½ cups uncooked long grain rice
⅓ cup chopped pine nuts or blanched almonds
⅓ cup currants or seedless raisins
1 teaspoon salt
¼ teaspoon pepper
1 pound chicken livers
1 tablespoon chopped fresh mint or parsley

Melt 2 tablespoons butter or margarine in a medium sized saucepan; add chicken broth; bring to a boil. Add rice, pine nuts or almonds, currants or raisins, salt, and pepper. Lower heat and cook slowly, covered, about 25 minutes, until rice is tender and liquid is absorbed. Meanwhile, sauté chicken livers in remaining 4 tablespoons butter or margarine in a medium sized skillet for 5 minutes, until tender. Spoon cooked rice into a buttered shallow baking dish. Top with chicken livers and butter drippings. Sprinkle top with mint or parsley. Cook in a preheated 400° oven 10 minutes. Serves 4.

Norwegian Cod-Vegetable Casserole

This is a nourishing casserole for a family supper.

3 large potatoes, cooked, peeled, and sliced
1½ cups cooked green peas
1 pound white-fleshed fish (cod or flounder) fillets,
*   cooked and cubed*
2 tablespoons fresh lemon juice
2 tablespoons all-purpose flour
4 tablespoons butter or margarine
2 cups light cream or milk
1 teaspoon dried thyme
3 tablespoons chopped fresh dill or parsley
1½ teaspoons salt
¼ teaspoon pepper
½ cup fine dry bread crumbs

Arrange half of the potato slices in a buttered shallow dish. Top with half the peas and half the fish cubes. Sprinkle with lemon juice. Repeat the layers. Stir flour into 2 tablespoons melted butter in a medium sized saucepan; blend well. Gradually add cream or milk, stirring as adding, and cook slowly, stirring, until thickened and smooth. Add thyme, dill or parsley, salt and pepper. Pour over vegetables and fish. Sprinkle with bread crumbs and remaining 2 tablespoons butter or margarine, melted. Bake in a preheated 350° oven 30 minutes, until ingredients are cooked and golden on top. Serves 6.

Balkan Lamb-Vegetable Casserole

Serve this hearty casserole for a company dinner.

2 pounds boneless lamb shoulder, cut into 1½-inch cubes
About 1½ cups olive or salad oil
2 medium-sized onions, peeled and chopped
1 teaspoon ground red pepper
2 teaspoons salt
½ teaspoon pepper
4 medium-sized potatoes, peeled and cubed
1 medium-sized eggplant, stemmed and cubed
3 large green peppers, cleaned and cut into strips
1½ cups fresh or frozen cut-up green beans
4 large tomatoes, peeled and sliced
3 eggs, beaten
¼ cup chopped fresh parsley

Wipe lamb cubes dry and brown on all sides in 3 tablespoons heated oil in a large saucepan. Remove to a plate. Add onions to drippings and sauté until tender. Add red pepper, salt, and pepper. Return lamb to saucepan. Add water to barely cover ingredients; cook slowly, covered, 1 hour. While lamb is cooking, sauté potatoes, eggplant, peppers, and green beans separately in oil. Or, omit this step and partially cook vegetables with the lamb. The dish will be more flavorful if the vegetables are sautéed separately in oil. Spoon lamb and other ingredients into a large shallow baking dish. Top with sautéed or partially cooked vegetables. Cook in a preheated 350° oven 1 hour, until ingredients are cooked. Put tomato slices over other vegetables 10 minutes before cooking is finished. Also combine eggs and parsley. Spoon over top of casserole, spreading evenly. Leave in oven long enough to set. Cool a little before serving. Serves 6 to 8.

Easy Turkey-Kidney Bean Casserole

This easy-to-prepare casserole can be made with leftover cooked turkey and canned beans. Serve for a family supper.

1 medium-sized onion, peeled and chopped
1 medium-sized carrot, scraped and diced
2 tablespoons butter or margarine
1 can (8 ounces) tomato sauce
2 teaspoons Worcestershire sauce
2 teaspoons prepared mustard
½ teaspoon crumbled dried rosemary
1½ teaspoons salt
¼ teaspoon pepper
1 can (16 ounces) kidney beans, drained
2 cups cubed cooked turkey

Sauté onion and carrot in heated butter or margarine in a saucepan for 5 minutes. Add tomato sauce, Worcestershire sauce, mustard, rosemary, salt, and pepper. Cook slowly, uncovered, for 10 minutes. Combine with beans and turkey in a shallow 1½-quart baking dish. Bake, covered, in a preheated 350° oven 30 minutes. Serves 4.

Italian Cheese-Filled Manicotti with Meat Sauce

This is a delectable casserole for an informal dinner party.

1 large onion, peeled and chopped
2 cloves garlic, crushed
2 tablespoons olive or salad oil
1 pound lean ground beef
1 can (1 pound, 12 ounces) Italian tomatoes, chopped
1 can (6 ounces) tomato paste
2 tomato paste cans water
2 teaspoons sugar
1 teaspoon dried oregano
½ teaspoon dried basil
⅔ cup chopped fresh parsley
1½ teaspoons salt
¼ teaspoon pepper
2 pounds ricotta or cottage cheese
½ pound mozzarella cheese, diced
½ cup grated Parmesan cheese
2 eggs, well beaten
1 tablespoon minced lemon rind
16 manicotti noodles, cooked

Sauté onion and garlic in heated oil in a large skillet until tender. Add beef and cook, stirring with a fork, until redness disappears. Add tomatoes, tomato paste, water, sugar, oregano, basil, ⅓ cup parsley, salt, and pepper. Cook slowly, uncovered, 45 minutes. Remove from heat. Combine cheeses, eggs, ½ cup parsley, and lemon rind in a large bowl. Season with salt and pepper, if desired. Stuff cooked manicotti noodles with the cheese filling, handling the manicotti carefully and with a small spoon pushing in the mixture to fill them completely. Allow some of the cheese mixture to protrude from both ends of the manicotti. Spoon half the meat sauce into a 3-quart shallow baking dish. Top with remaining sauce. Sprinkle with grated Parmesan cheese, if desired. Bake in a preheated 350° oven 30 minutes. Serves 8.

Old-Fashioned Baked Corned Beef Hash with Eggs

This is a good hearty dish for a Sunday brunch.

1 medium-sized onion, peeled and chopped
2 tablespoons butter or margarine
2 cans (12 ounces each) corned beef, coarsely chopped
4 medium-sized potatoes, boiled, peeled, and diced
1 medium-sized green pepper, cleaned and chopped
½ teaspoon salt
½ teapoon pepper
¾ cup tomato juice
6 eggs
⅓ cup chopped fresh parsley

Sauté onion in heated butter or margarine in a large skillet until tender. Add corned beef, potatoes, green pepper, salt, and pepper. Mix well and fry 2 or 3 minutes. Spoon into a shallow baking dish. Top with tomato juice. Bake, uncovered, 25 minutes. Make 6 indentations in top of hash with back of a large spoon. Break an egg into each indentation. Bake about 12 minutes longer, until eggs are just set. Serve at once. Serves 6.

French Mushroom-Filled Pancakes

This is an attractive entrée for a ladies' luncheon.

1 medium-sized onion, peeled and minced
About 5 tablespoons butter or margarine
1 pound fresh mushrooms, cleaned and chopped
2 tablespoons all-purpose flour
½ cup sour cream, at room temperature
2 tablespoons chopped fresh dill or parsley
Salt, pepper to taste
⅛ teaspoon grated nutmeg
1 cup light cream or milk
1 egg, beaten
1 cup sifted all-purpose flour
¼ cup grated Parmesan cheese

Sauté onion in 3 tablespoons heated butter or margarine in a medium sized skillet until tender. Add mushrooms; sauté 5 minutes. Mix in 2 tablespoons flour and cook 1 minute. Add sour cream, dill or parsley, salt and pepper to taste, and nutmeg. Cook slowly, stirring, 1 or 2 minutes. Remove from heat and cool. Combine cream or milk, egg, and 1 cup flour in a bowl. Season with salt. When well blended, pour 3 or 4 tablespoons butter into a heated lightly greased 7- or 8-inch skillet. Tilt at once to spread evenly. Cook until golden on one side. Turn and cook on other side. Keep pancakes warm in a preheated 250° oven while cooking other pancakes. Put about 2 large tablespoons of mushroom mixture onto each pancake. Roll up and arrange, seam side down, in a buttered shallow baking dish. Dot top with butter and sprinkle with grated cheese. Bake in a preheated 400° oven about 10 minutes, until hot and golden on top. Serves 4 to 6.

Italian Green Noodle Lasagne

This is a special entrée to serve for a company dinner. The green noodles are baked with a wine flavored meat sauce.

½ cup butter or margarine
1 cup minced onion
1 medium-sized carrot, scraped and diced
1 medium-sized stalk celery, diced
1 garlic clove, crushed
1 pound lean ground beef
1 can (10½ ounces) tomato purée
1 cup beef bouillon
⅓ cup Marsala wine
1 teaspoon dried marjoram
Salt, pepper to taste
⅓ cup chopped fresh parsley
2 tablespoons all-purpose flour
2½ cups light cream or milk
⅛ teaspoon grated nutmeg
¾ pound broad green or spinach noodles
1 cup grated Parmesan cheese

Heat ¼ cup butter or margarine in a large skillet. Add onion, carrot, celery, and garlic and sauté 5 minutes. Add beef and cook, stirring with a fork, until redness disappears. Add tomato purée, ½ cup beef bouillon, Marsala, and marjoram. Season with salt and pepper. Simmer, uncovered, 1 hour. Gradually add remaining ½ cup bouillon and cook another 30 minutes. Add parsley and remove from heat. The final sauce should be thick. Melt 2 tablespoons butter or margarine in a medium sized saucepan. Stir in flour; cook 1 minute. Gradually add cream or milk, stirring as adding. Cook slowly, stirring, until thickened and smooth. Season with salt and pepper. Add nutmeg. Remove from heat. Cook noodles according to package directions until just tender; drain. Turn noodles into a bowl and mix with 2 tablespoons butter or margarine to keep from sticking together. To assemble ingredients, spoon a thin layer of meat sauce over surface of a 3-quart shallow baking dish. Add a layer of cooked noodles and then layers of meat sauce and cream sauce and a sprinkling of grated cheese. Repeat to use all ingredients, sprinkling top with a generous layer of grated cheese. Bake, uncovered, in a preheated 350° oven 25 minutes, until hot and bubbly and top is golden. Serves 6 to 8.

Chicken Tetrazzini

This well-known pasta casserole can be made with leftover cooked chicken or turkey. Serve for an informal luncheon or supper.

1 large onion, peeled and minced
2 tablespoons butter or margarine
1 cup sliced fresh or canned mushrooms
2 tablespoons fresh lemon juice
Salt, pepper to taste
⅛ teaspoon grated nutmeg
1 can (10½ ounces) condensed cream of mushroom soup
1 can (10½ ounces) condensed golden mushroom soup
2 soup cans light cream or milk
1 cup grated American cheese
¼ cup dry sherry
1 pound spaghettini
4 cups slivered cooked chicken or turkey
4 large fresh mushrooms, cleaned and sliced lengthwise

Sauté onion in heated butter or margarine in a large saucepan until tender. Add sliced fresh or canned mushrooms and lemon juice; sauté 4 minutes, if fresh, and 2 minutes, if canned. Season with salt and pepper. Add nutmeg. Add canned soups and cream and mix well. Heat gently, stirring. Mix in cheese and leave on low heat until cheese melts. Remove from heat and stir in sherry. Cook spaghettini according to package directions; drain. Spoon half spaghettini into a buttered 3-quart shallow baking dish, spreading evenly. Cover with chicken or turkey. Add remaining spaghettini, spreading evenly. Pour sauce over ingredients. Arrange sliced mushrooms over top of dish. Bake, uncovered, in a preheated 375° oven 30 minutes, until hot and bubbly and top is golden. Serves 6 to 8.

Stews and Ragouts

For taste tempting, appealing main dishes, you can't beat these stews and ragouts, which are particularly appropriate for special occasion family or company meals.

Too often a stew is considered merely a mixture of any available ingredients thrown into a pot and dished up in a mood of culinary abandon or desperation. Unfortunately, this practice is sometimes followed, but it ignores the fact that stews are actually gastronomic treasures created in many countries with a wide but selective number of interesting ingredients. Such dishes are an integral part of the cook's repertoire and can be proudly served on any occasion.

Taken from the French word *ragouter,* meaning "to revive the taste," a ragout denotes a stew that is generally highly seasoned, perhaps with wine, spices, or other flavorings. Although primarily thought of as a French dish, other cuisines have evolved notable ragouts prepared with meat, game, poultry or fish, and sometimes with vegetables.

The earliest stews were indeed haphazard and were made

217

with pieces of meat or game, legumes, and perhaps other vegetables, and seasonings. They provided necessary sustenance. Trying to improve them, the Romans cooked bizarre mixtures that were so heavily spiced that the taste of the basic foods was overpowered. Nevertheless, they did create early versions of fricassees and ragouts.

We are indebted to the French for refining the preparation of stews. As early as the twelfth century French chefs had succeeded in converting basic dishes to more sophisticated fare and bequeathed to the culinary world a glorious repertoire of *blanquettes, daubes, navarins, matelotes,* fricassees, and ragouts.

Almost every other country has contributed one or more favorite stews. Cooks everywhere created such well-known dishes as goulashes, or the ubiquitous Mediterranean stew known variously as *stifado, estofado,* or *estouffade.* Less familiar, but equally intriguing, are the Philippine *adobo* and the West African *jollof.* One could not make a culinary tour of the world without sampling these national dishes.

Basically, stews are made by covering the food with liquid and slowly cooking in a tightly covered heavy pot or casserole either over direct heat or in the oven. The cooking is generally lengthy as the purpose is to tenderize the foods and make them more palatable by retaining the juices. Meat stews are either brown or white. For the former the meat is browned before cooking in liquid, while for the latter it is not. Stews generally have thick rich sauces derived from slow cooking or from the addition of thickening agents.

The cuts of meat used for stews may vary from less tender and less expensive beef shank and short ribs to more tender and more expensive beef sirloin and veal shoulder. Meats and other ingredients, however, should be of prime quality. The finer the quality of the ingredients, the better the dish can be.

Various pots, kettles, or casseroles may be used. The cooking utensil should be heavy and large, with a tight-fitting cover. Determine if the container can be used for cooking over direct heat (or on top of the stove) as well as in the oven. Some utensils are suitable for both types of cookery; others are not.

The preferable utensil is a flame-proof, heavy-bottomed pan, kettle or casserole. Pans made of heavy copper or enameled cast iron are best because they retain the heat during the long, slow cooking process; they also help keep the food from burning. Special dishes that can be purchased in some department stores or gourmet shops include the French enameled cast iron *cocottes* and earthenware or metal *daubières*.

For the best results, great care should be accorded the preparation and cooking of each dish. If the meat is to be browned, it should first be wiped dry so that it does not steam. Add only a few pieces at a time and keep them separate while browning. Do not pierce the meat with a fork while it is cooking lest desirable juices be lost. After a preliminary browning, some stews are deglazed by flaming with a liquor such as brandy, before the addition of the primary liquid and other ingredients.

The most important step in stewing meat or other foods is to dissolve the food juices in the hot liquid. Thus the first step in cooking a stew is very important. The liquid should be slowly heated to the point where it simmers, bubbling occasionally. It is then left to cook as slowly as possible. This is important because if the liquid boils the meat will become tough and lose its proper taste. All meat shrinks while cooking, but lower temperatures reduce the loss. The length of the cooking time will vary with the type and cut of meat, but the best way to ensure that it is properly done is to test it. Since it is not possible to specify precise cooking times, those in the following recipes are suggested as guidelines.

Vegetables and other foods are added to stews at various intervals during the cooking. Generally they require less time than meats and should not be overdone or they will lose their shape and color. To improve the flavor of some stews, vegetables or other seasonings are first sautéed in fat.

Once a stew has cooked, remove any fat that has collected on the surface. While the liquid is till hot you may do this with a slotted spoon, a skimmer, or pieces of paper toweling. Alternatively, you may cool and refrigerate the dish and then lift off the solidified fat.

For some stews it may be necessary to correct the final sauce by thinning it with more stock, wine or other liquid. On the other hand, the sauce can be thickened by boiling down or adding *beurre manie* (tiny balls of flour and butter), cornstarch, arrowroot, or egg yolks and cream. If a stew is to be refrigerated or frozen, it is advisable to adjust the sauce after it has been reheated. Stews are not difficult to reheat, but should be checked so that none of the ingredients becomes overdone and loses its proper form and color.

It's great fun to entertain with stews and ragouts as you'll see from the following selection of international recipes. They are perfect for buffets, dinners or suppers, as well as day time meals, and they generate an air of camaraderie, whether the service is formal or informal.

Belgian Beef Stew with Beer

This hearty beef stew, flavored with beer, brown sugar, and herbs, is traditional fare in Belgium's northern region of Flanders. It is called *carbonnade à la Flamande*. The name is believed to have derived from the French word for carbon which means broiled or grilled over coals or carbon. Serve for a winter dinner.

> *3 pounds lean boneless beef chuck, cut into 1-inch cubes*
> *⅓ cup all-purpose flour*
> *2½ teaspoons salt*
> *¾ teaspoon pepper*
> *4 large onions, peeled and sliced thin*

2 cloves garlic, crushed
½ cup shortening, butter or margarine
2 medium bay leaves
1 teaspoon dried thyme
4 sprigs parsley
3 tablespoons brown sugar
About 2½ cups light beer
6 medium-sized potatoes, peeled and halved
2 tablespoons red wine vinegar

Wipe beef cubes dry and sprinkle with flour, seasoned with salt and pepper. Set aside. Sauté onions and garlic in heated shortening in a large saucepan. Remove to a plate. Add beef cubes, several at a time, and brown on all sides. Return onions and garlic to kettle. Tie bay leaves, thyme and parsley in a square of cheesecloth to form a *bouquet garni*. Add, with sugar and beer, to beef mixture. Cook slowly, tightly covered, for 1½ hours. Add potatoes and continue cooking another 25 minutes, until ingredients are tender. Add a little more beer during cooking, if needed. Remove and discard *bouquet garni*. Add vinegar just before removing from heat. Serves 8.

Key West Piccadillo

This flavorful ground beef stew containing raisins and capers originated in Cuba but is popular fare in the Florida Keys. It is served with or over cooked white rice and is a good luncheon specialty.

1 large onion, peeled and chopped
2 cloves garlic, crushed
2 tablespoons salad oil
3 medium-sized tomatoes, peeled and chopped

   1 pound ground beef
   1 teaspoon salt
   ¼ teaspoon pepper
   1 large green pepper, cleaned and cubed
   ½ cup raisins, previously plumped in warm water
   2 tablespoons drained capers or sliced green olives
   2 cups hot cooked long grain rice

   Sauté onion and garlic in heated oil in a medium sized skillet until tender. Add tomatoes; cook 1 minute. Add beef and continue cooking, stirring with a fork, until redness disappears. Add salt and pepper. Cook slowly, covered, 20 minutes, stirring occasionally. Add green pepper, raisins, and capers. Continue cooking another 10 minutes. Serve over hot rice in wide soup bowls or on plates. Serves 4.

Tunisian Lamb Couscous

   A specialty of North African and Southern European countries is a flavorful stew called couscous, made with a grain of the same name, vegetables, meat or poultry, and seasonings. Traditionally the stew is cooked in a *couscoussière*, a sort of large double boiler with a perforated top placed over a bottom kettle. Couscous can be purchased in some supermarkets and specialty food stores. This is a good buffet dish.

   1 cup chick-peas
   1 package (500 grams or 17 ounces) couscous
   3 pounds lean lamb, leg or shoulder, cut into 2-inch
      cubes
   About ⅓ cup olive or salad oil
   2 large onions, peeled and chopped
   1 can (6 ounces) tomato paste

1 teaspoon ground red pepper
½ teaspoon ground cumin
2 teaspoons salt
½ teaspoon pepper
10 cups water or beef bouillon
3 large carrots, scraped and sliced thick
2 medium-sized zucchini, washed, stemmed and sliced
   thick
2 medium-sized white turnips, peeled and cubed
1 large green pepper, cleaned and cut into strips
½ cup chopped fresh coriander or parsley

Soak chick-peas in water to cover overnight. Spread couscous on a large tray or platter; sprinkle with enough water to dampen it and mix with the hands. Wipe lamb cubes dry and brown, several at a time, in heated oil in a *couscoussière* or large kettle. Remove to a plate. Add onions to drippings; sauté until tender. Stir in tomato paste, red pepper, cumin, salt, and pepper. Add water or bouillon; bring to a boil. Return lamb to saucepan. Add chick-peas and lower heat. Cook slowly, covered, 30 minutes. Add carrots, zucchini, turnips, and green pepper to stew. Put couscous in top of cooker, or in a colander lined with cheesecloth, and place over kettle. Continue cooking about 30 minutes longer, until couscous and stew ingredients are cooked. Stir in coriander or parsley. To serve, spoon couscous onto a large platter and arrange lamb and vegetables around it. Sprinkle some of chick-peas and sauce over top as a garnish. Serves 8 to 10.

Note: Canned chick-peas can be used, if desired. If so, it will not be necessary to soak them overnight. Drain before using.

Polish Bigos

Bigos, a traditional Polish hunters' stew, was originally made in great quantity with various leftover cooked meats and game, vegetables, and fruit. This version is excellent for a winter buffet.

2 ounces dried brown mushrooms
¼ pound salt pork or bacon, diced
3 large onions, peeled and sliced thin
½ pound (about 2½ cups) shredded green cabbage
1 pound lean beef, cut into 1½-inch cubes
1 pound lean pork, cut into 1½-inch cubes
3 pounds sauerkraut, washed and drained
3 medium-sized tart apples, peeled, cored, and chopped
1 can (14½ ounces) whole tomatoes, undrained
1 cup vegetable broth or water
2 teaspoons sugar
2 teaspoons prepared sharp mustard
1 tablespoon salt
¾ teaspoon pepper
1 pound smoked Polish sausage or kielbasa, *cut into 1-inch rounds*
½ cup Madeira wine
12 medium-sized potatoes, peeled and boiled
¼ cup chopped fresh parsley.

Soak mushrooms in lukewarm water in a small bowl 20 minutes. Drain, reserving mushroom liquid. Press mushrooms to release all liquid; chop and set aside. Fry salt pork or bacon and onions in a large kettle until onions are tender. Add cabbage and sauté 3 minutes. Push aside. Wipe beef and pork dry. Put in kettle and brown on all sides; mix ingredients. Add sauerkraut, apples, tomatoes, mushrooms and reserved liquid, vegetable broth, sugar, mustard, salt, and pepper. Cook slowly, covered, about 2 hours, until ingredients are tender. Add sausage during last 30 minutes of cooking. Stir in Madeira just before removing from heat. Add potatoes to stew or serve separately garnished with parsley. Serves 12.

Note: Substitute 1 cup sliced fresh or canned mushrooms for the dried ones, if desired. Add during last 15 minutes of cooking.

Moroccan Chicken Stew with Olives

In the North African country of Morocco excellent stews of many variations are cooked in a glazed earthenware casserole calleda *tajine*. The stew is also named *tajine*. Although traditionally made with pickled lemons, fresh lemons are used in this recipe.

> *3 medium-sized onions, peeled and sliced thin*
> *2–3 garlic cloves, crushed*
> *About ⅓ cup olive or salad oil*
> *2 teaspoons ground ginger*
> *2 teaspoons ground coriander*
> *¼ cup chopped fresh coriander or parsley*
> *1 tablespoon salt*
> *¾ teaspoon pepper*
> *2 broiler-fryer chickens, about 2½ pounds each, cut up*
> *1½ cups chicken broth or water*
> *2 medium-sized lemons, quartered*
> *1 cup pitted green olives*

Sauté onions and garlic in heated oil in a large kettle until tender. Add ginger, coriander, fresh coriander or parsley, salt, and pepper; cook 2 minutes. Wipe chicken dry and fry, a few pieces at a time, until golden on all sides, adding more oil if needed. Add broth or water. Bring to a boil. Lower heat and cook slowly, covered, 30 minutes. Add lemons and olives and continue cooking another 20 minutes, until ingredients are tender. Serves 6 to 8.

Burgoo from Kentucky

This famous southern stew has long been served in Kentucky at outdoor gatherings such as political rallies or holiday celebrations. It takes considerable time to prepare and includes a number of ingredients, but it will serve a large gathering either outdoors or indoors.

> *4 pounds mixed meat (pork, beef, veal and/or lamb)*
> *shanks*
> *1 roasting or stewing chicken, about 4 pounds*
> *1 tablespoon salt*
> *2 teaspoons pepper*
> *4 large potatoes, peeled and cubed*
> *3 large carrots, scraped and chopped*
> *2 large onions, peeled and chopped*
> *2 cups shredded green cabbage*
> *2 cups fresh or frozen corn kernels*
> *3 large tomatoes, peeled and chopped*
> *1 package (10 ounces) frozen lima beans*
> *1 package (10 ounces) frozen whole okra*
> *2 tablespoons Worcestershire sauce*
> *2 large green peppers, cleaned and chopped*

Put meat shanks and chicken into a large kettle. Add enough water to just cover them. Add salt and pepper. Lower heat and cook slowly, covered, 1½ hours, until meat and chicken are tender. Remove from kettle; cut all meat from bones and cut into bite-size pieces; return to kettle. Discard any skin and bones. Heat to boiling. Lower heat and add vegetables except lima beans, okra, and green peppers. Cook slowly, covered, 20 minutes. Add remaining ingredients and continue cooking about 20 minutes longer, until ingredients are tender. Serve in an extra large bowl or kettle. Ladle into large cups or soup plates. Serves 16.

South American Beef-Fruit Stew

This hearty stew called *carbonada Criolla* is an intriguing combination of beef, fruit, and vegetables. Serve for a winter dinner.

1 large onion, peeled and chopped
2 cloves garlic, crushed
¼ cup vegetable oil
2 pounds lean stew beef, cut into 1½-inch cubes
1 can (1 pound) tomatoes, chopped
1 bay leaf
1 teaspoon dried oregano
1½ teaspoons salt
¼ teaspoon pepper
2 cups beef bouillon
3 medium-sized sweet potatoes, peeled and cubed
2 cups cubed butternut or acorn squash
1 large green pepper, cleaned and cut into strips
1 cup fresh or frozen corn
1 cup diced fresh or canned peaches
1 medium-sized tart apple, pared, cored, and diced

Sauté onion and garlic in heated oil in a large kettle until tender. Wipe beef cubes dry and brown, several at a time, on all sides. Add tomatoes, bay leaf, oregano, salt, and pepper; cook 1 minute. Pour in bouillon and bring to a boil. Lower heat and cook slowly, covered, 1½ hours. Add potatoes and squash; continue cooking another 25 minutes, until vegetables are just tender. Add remaining ingredients and cook about 10 minutes longer, allowing more time for fresh than frozen corn. Serves 6.

Hungarian Pork-Paprika Stew

In Hungary a paprika flavored pork or beef stew for which the meat is cut into strips is called a *tokany*. It is richly flavored with sour cream and mushrooms. Serve for an early or late evening dinner.

> *2 pounds lean boneless pork, cut into 3x1-inch strips*
> *⅓ cup lard or shortening*
> *1–2 tablespoons paprika, preferably Hungarian*
> *1½ teaspoons salt*
> *½ teaspoon pepper*
> *1 large onion, peeled and chopped*
> *2 cups water*
> *1 large carrot, scraped and sliced thin*
> *1 large green pepper, cleaned and cubed*
> *2 medium-sized tomatoes, peeled and chopped*
> *2 cups sliced mushrooms*
> *1 tablespoon all-purpose flour*
> *1 cup sour cream at room temperature*

Wipe pork strips dry and brown, several at a time, in heated lard or shortening in a large saucepan or kettle. Add paprika, salt, and pepper; cook 1 minute. Push aside and add onion; sauté until tender. Add water and bring to a boil. Lower heat and cook slowly, covered, 1 hour. Add carrot, green pepper, tomatoes, and mushrooms; continue cooking 30 minutes, until pork and vegetables are tender. Combine flour and sour cream; stir into stew. Cook over low heat, stirring, until thickened and smooth, about 5 minutes. Serves 6.

Armenian Veal-Cracked Wheat Stew

This creative stew is made with inexpensive veal shanks and neck pieces and cracked wheat or bulgur, a delicious nutty flavored grain used as a staple in the Middle East and some neighboring areas. Serve this stew for a weekend luncheon or supper.

2 pounds veal shanks
1½ to 2 pounds veal neck pieces
About ¼ cup butter or salad oil
1 medium-sized onion, peeled and chopped
2 cloves garlic, crushed
2 cups beef bouillon
1½ teaspoons salt
¼ teaspoon pepper
1 cup cracked wheat (bulgur)
1 can (10½ ounces) tomato purée
1 jar (1 pound) small white onions, undrained
1 cup sliced fresh or canned mushrooms
½ teaspoon dried marjoram

Wash and wipe veal shanks and neck pieces dry. Brown on all sides in heated butter or oil in a large kettle. Remove to a plate. Add onion and garlic to drippings; sauté until tender. Add veal shanks and neck pieces, bouillon, salt, and pepper. Bring to a boil. Lower heat and cook slowly, covered, 1½ hours. Meanwhile, cook cracked wheat in 2 cups water about 25 minutes, until grains are tender and liquid has been absorbed. When meat has cooked 1½ hours, add tomato purée, onions, mushrooms, marjoram, and cooked cracked wheat. Cook another 10 minutes. Serves 6 to 8.

Corsican Wine-Flavored Beef Stew

On the rugged French island of Corsica there are many hearty stews. This one, called *pebronata de boeuf*, is superb for a late evening party.

> *2 large onions, peeled and chopped*
> *3 cloves garlic, crushed*
> *⅔ cup olive or salad oil*
> *2 bay leaves, crumbled*
> *1 teaspoon dried thyme*
> *1 tablespoon salt*
> *¾ teaspoon pepper*
> *5 pounds boneless lean beef, cut into 1½-inch cubes*
> *¼ cup all-purpose flour*
> *2 cups dry red wine*
> *1 to 2 teaspoons ground red pepper*
> *1 cup tomato sauce*
> *1 teaspoon dried oregano*

Sauté onions and garlic in heated oil in a large kettle until tender. Add bay leaves, thyme, salt, and pepper; cook 1 minute. Wipe beef cubes dry and brown, several at a time, on all sides. Sprinkle with flour and mix well. Add wine. Bring to a boil. Lower heat and cook slowly, covered, 1½ hours. Add red pepper, the amount according to taste, tomato sauce, and oregano.

Continue to cook slowly another 30 minutes, until meat is tender. The final sauce should be quite thick. Serves 12.

Maine "Joe Booker" Stew

This substantial beef and vegetable stew, sometimes served with dumplings, has long been a favorite dish in Boothbay Harbor, Maine. No one seems to know anything about "Joe Booker" or how the stew received its name. A good dish for a winter supper.

> ½ pound salt pork, diced
> 2 pounds lean beef chuck or veal, cut into 1-inch cubes
> 2 medium-sized onions, peeled and sliced
> 6 cups water
> ½ teaspoon salt
> ½ teaspoon pepper
> 2 cups diced peeled potatoes
> 2 cups diced scraped carrots
> 2 cups diced peeled turnips

Fry salt pork in a large kettle to render all the fat. Remove pork and discard. Wipe meat cubes dry and brown, several at a time, in heated fat on all sides. Remove to a plate. Add onions to drippings; sauté until tender. Return meat cubes to kettle. Add water, salt, and pepper. Bring to a boil. Lower heat and cook slowly, covered, for 1½ hours. Add vegetables and continue to cook another 30 minutes, until meat and vegetables are tender. Serves 6 to 8.

Portuguese Pork-Clam Stew

This is an unusual stew to serve for a company weekend luncheon.

2 pounds lean boneless pork, cut into small cubes
3 tablespoons olive or salad oil
2 large onions, peeled and sliced thin
2 cloves garlic, crushed
4 large tomatoes, peeled and chopped
1 can (6 ounces) tomato paste
1½ cups dry white wine
1 teaspoon paprika
1½ teaspoons salt
½ teaspoon pepper
2 dozen hard shelled clams, scrubbed and washed
⅓ cup chopped fresh parsley

Wipe pork cubes dry and brown, several at a time, in heated oil in a large kettle. Remove to a plate. Add onions and garlic to drippings; sauté until tender. Return pork cubes to kettle. Add tomatoes and cook 2 minutes. Stir in tomato paste, wine, paprika, salt, and pepper; mix well. Bring to a boil. Lower heat and cook slowly, covered, 1½ hours, until pork is tender. Add clams and continue cooking until shells open, about 15 minutes. Mix in parsley. Serves 6.

Spanish Cocido

Cocido is the Spanish national dish and is subject to both regional and individual variations. This version of the meat and

vegetable stew includes chick-peas and rice. It is an excellent
entrée for a buffet.

1 large onion, peeled and chopped
3 tablespoons olive or salad oil
1 pound stew beef, cut into 2-inch cubes
2 pounds beef soup bones with marrow
¼ pound bacon in one piece
2 quarts water
2 teaspoons salt
½ teaspoon pepper
1 large carrot, scraped and diced
1 can (1 pound, 4 ounces) chick-peas, drained
3 large tomatoes, peeled and cut up
¾ cup uncooked long grain rice
1 pound Spanish sausage (chorizo) or garlic sausage,
   sliced thin
⅛ to ¼ teaspoon ground red pepper
2 cups frozen cut-up green beans
Pinch saffron (optional)

Sauté onion in heated oil in a large kettle until tender. Push
aside. Wipe beef cubes dry and brown, several at a time, on all
sides. Add beef bones, bacon, water, salt, and pepper. Bring to a
boil. Lower heat and cook slowly, covered, 1½ hours. Remove
cover and skim off any fat that has accumulated on top. Add
carrot and cook 15 minutes. Stir in chick-peas, tomatoes, rice,
sausage, and red pepper. Continue cooking about 20 minutes
longer, until ingredients are tender. Add green beans 10 minutes
before cooking is finished. Stir in saffron before removing from
heat. Remove bones and take out any marrow left in them.
Return marrow to stew and discard bones. Serves 6.

Western Chuck Wagon Beef-Bean Stew

This easy-to-prepare ground beef and pinto bean stew can be served for an outdoor supper.

1 pound dried pinto beans
4 cups water
2 large onions, peeled and chopped
2 cloves garlic, crushed
2 tablespoons shortening or salad oil
2 pounds ground beef
1 teaspoon dried oregano
1 tablespoon chili powder
½ teaspoon ground cumin
1 can (1 pound) tomatoes, chopped

Put beans and water into a large kettle; bring to a boil and boil 2 minutes. Remove from heat and let stand, covered, 1 hour. Meanwhile, sauté onions and garlic in heated shortening or oil in a large skillet until tender. Add beef and cook, mixing with a fork, until redness disappears. Remove from heat. Cook beans in water 1 hour. Add ground beef mixture and remaining ingredients; mix well. Continue to cook about 45 minutes longer, until beans are tender. Serves 10 to 12.

Greek Beef Stifado

Restaurants, or *tavernas,* in Greece are noted for their superb traditional cookery such as this wine flavored beef stew. It is a good dish for an informal buffet and may be served over cooked white rice.

4 pounds boneless beef chuck or stew meat, cut into 1½-inch cubes

⅔ cup olive or salad oil, or combination of both

4 pounds small white onions, peeled

1 can (6 ounces) tomato paste

1½ cups dry red wine

3 to 4 cloves garlic, peeled and halved

1 stick cinnamon or 2 teaspoons ground cinnamon

6 whole cloves

2 bay leaves

1 tablespoon salt

¾ teaspoon pepper

Wipe beef cubes dry. Brown, several at a time, in ½ cup heated oil in a large kettle. Take kettle off heat and set aside. Sauté onions in remaining oil in a large skillet until golden on all sides. Spoon, with drippings, over beef cubes. Do not mix together. Combine tomato paste and red wine; pour over beef and onions. Add remaining ingredients. Cook very slowly, tightly covered, about 2 hours, until beef is tender, adding a little water, if needed. The final sauce should be quite thick and will be better if cooked very slowly. Discard garlic, cinnamon sticks, cloves, and bay leaves before serving. Serves 12.

French Lamb-Vegetable Stew

A marvelous French specialty called *navarin printanier* is made with lamb and a variety of fresh spring vegetables, but frozen ones may be used, if desired. Although generally baked in the oven, the stew can be cooked on top of the stove. It is an excellent dish for a company dinner.

3 pounds lean lamb shoulder, cut into 2-inch cubes
¼ cup butter or salad oil
1 tablespoon sugar
2 teaspoons salt
½ teaspoon pepper
2 tablespoons all-purpose flour
2 cups beef bouillon or water
4 medium-sized tomatoes, seeded, peeled, and chopped
2 cloves garlic, crushed
1 bay leaf
½ teaspoon dried thyme
6 medium-sized carrots, scraped and sliced thick
6 small white turnips, peeled and cubed
12 small new potatoes or 6 medium-sized potatoes,
*   peeled and cubed*
16 small white onions, peeled
1 cup shelled fresh or frozen green peas
1 cup cut-up fresh or frozen green beans

Wipe lamb cubes dry. Brown, several at a time, on all sides in heated butter or oil in a large kettle. Add sugar and leave over moderately high heat until it caramelizes, about 5 minutes. Add salt and pepper. Sprinkle with flour and mix well. Add bouillon or water, tomatoes, garlic, bay leaf, and thyme. Mix well and bring to a boil. Lower heat and cook slowly, covered, 1 hour. Take off stove and spoon meat onto a plate. Strain sauce into a bowl. Wash kettle in which meat was cooked; return strained sauce and meat to it. Add carrots, turnips, potatoes, and onions. Cook slowly, covered, about 40 minutes, until lamb and vegetables are tender. Add peas and green beans during last 20 minutes, if fresh, or 10 minutes, if frozen, of cooking. Serves 8.

Philippine Pork-Chicken Stew

Filipinos serve this traditional stew called *adobo* at holiday meals or for festive family get-togethers. It is a good dish for an outdoor meal.

> 1 broiler-fryer chicken, about 2½ pounds, cut up
> 2 pounds boneless pork loin or shoulder, cut into 1-inch cubes
> 1 cup wine vinegar
> ½ cup soy sauce
> 2 bay leaves
> 2 garlic cloves, halved
> 1 teaspoon peppercorns, slightly bruised
> About 3 tablespoons lard or peanut oil
> 1 cup coconut milk (recipe below)

Put chicken pieces, pork, vinegar, soy sauce, bay leaves, garlic, and peppercorns into a large kettle. Leave to marinate, covered, at room temperature for 1½ to 2 hours. Put chicken-pork mixture on stove; bring to a boil. Lower heat and cook slowly, about 1½ hours, until chicken and pork are tender. Remove chicken and pork; drain on paper toweling. Strain and reserve liquid. Fry chicken and pork on all sides in heated lard or oil in a kettle. Return liquid to kettle. Add coconut milk and cook slowly, uncovered, about 15 minutes, until mixture thickens a little. Serves 8.

Note: The cooking time is for a very low heat. Use less time if not possible to maintain the very low heat.

Coconut Milk

Put 1 cup freshly grated or packaged or frozen unsweetened coconut and 1 cup hot water in a bowl. Leave 20 minutes. Strain liquid from coconut, discarding coconut. Use as "milk" as directed in above recipe.

French Beef Bourguignon

This well-known traditional French stew, flavored with wine and including onions and mushrooms, is an excellent entrée for a weekend buffet or dinner party.

> *5 pounds boneless stewing beef, cut into 1½-inch cubes*
> *½ cup diced bacon or salt pork*
> *About 6 tablespoons olive or salad oil*
> *2 medium-sized carrots, scraped and diced*
> *2 medium-sized onions, peeled and chopped*
> *3 tablespoons all-purpose flour*
> *3 to 4 cloves garlic, crushed*
> *2 bay leaves*
> *4 sprigs parsley*
> *1 teaspoon dried thyme*
> *2 cups dry red wine*
> *2 cups beef stock or bouillon*
> *1 tablespoon salt*
> *¾ teaspoon pepper*
> *24 small white onions, peeled*
> *About ½ cup butter or margarine*
> *24 fresh mushrooms, cleaned*
> *2 tablespoons tomato paste*

Wipe beef cubes dry. Fry bacon or salt pork in a large kettle.

Add oil and heat. Add beef cubes, several at a time, and brown on all sides. Remove to a plate. Add carrots and onions to drippings; sauté 5 minutes. Return beef to kettle. Sprinkle with flour and mix well. Add garlic, bay leaves, parsley, thyme, wine, stock or bouillon, salt, and pepper. Bring to a boil. Lower heat and cook slowly, covered, 2 hours, until meat is tender. While stew is cooking, sauté onions in ¼ cup butter in a saucepan until golden. Add water to cover and cook, covered, about 12 minutes, until just tender. Cut mushrooms in half lengthwise and sauté in remaining butter, adding more if needed, in a skillet for 4 minutes. Add tomato paste to stew 10 minutes before cooking is finished. Add onions and mushrooms, with drippings, just before removing from the heat. Serves 12.

West African Jollof

In West Africa a typical stew called *jollof* is made with chicken and/or meat, vegetables, rice, and spicy seasonings. It is a good entrée for a weekend luncheon or supper.

½ pound salt pork, diced
About 4 tablespoons peanut or salad oil
1 pound boneless stew beef, cut into 1½-inch cubes
2 broiler-fryer chickens, about 2½ pounds each, cut up
3 large onions, peeled and sliced thin
4 large tomatoes, peeled and sliced thin
2 large green peppers, cleaned and cut into strips
2 bay leaves
1–2 teaspoons ground red pepper
1 teaspoon dried thyme
1 tablespoon salt
½ teaspoon pepper
2 cans (6 ounces each) tomato paste

> *1 cup water*
> *1 tablespoon fresh lemon juice*
> *2 cups chicken broth*
> *2 cups uncooked long grain rice*

Put salt pork and oil into a large kettle; fry pork until most of fat is rendered. Wipe beef cubes dry with paper toweling; brown, several at a time, on all sides in heated fat and oil. Remove to a plate. Wipe chicken pieces dry; fry, several at a time, until golden on all sides, adding more oil, if needed. Remove to a plate. Add onions to drippings; sauté until tender. Add tomatoes and green peppers; cook 2 minutes. Add bay leaves, red pepper, thyme, salt, pepper, tomato paste, water, and lemon juice; mix well. Cook 5 minutes. Return beef and chicken to kettle. Add chicken broth; bring to a boil. Lower heat and cook slowly, covered, 45 minutes. Add rice and continue to cook slowly, covered, about 30 minutes, until beef and chicken are tender and almost all liquid has been absorbed by the rice. Serves 10.

French Veal Blanquette

One of the best French stews is a meat or poultry dish with a lemon flavored cream sauce called a *blanquette*. Additional ingredients are small white onions and mushrooms. Serve this elegant entrée for a company dinner.

> *2½ pounds boneless veal shoulder, cut into 2-inch cubes*
> *4 cups beef bouillon or water*
> *1 large carrot, scraped and chopped*
> *1 medium-sized onion stuck with 2 whole cloves*
> *1 leek, white part only, cleaned and sliced*
> *1 bouquet garni (1 bay leaf, ½ teaspoon dried thyme, 2*
> * sprigs parsley)*

2 teaspoons salt
¼ teaspoon pepper
5 tablespoons butter or margarine
16 small white onions, peeled
½ cup water
18 medium-sized fresh mushrooms, cleaned and halved
    lengthwise
2 tablespoons fresh lemon juice
3 tablespoons all-purpose flour
2 egg yolks
½ cup heavy cream
Freshly grated nutmeg to taste

Put veal cubes and bouillon or water in a large kettle. Bring to a boil; skim. Add carrot, onion with cloves, leek, *bouquet garni*, salt, and pepper. Lower heat and cook slowly, covered, 1½ hours, skimming once or twice. Meanwhile, melt 1 tablespoon butter or margarine in a medium sized saucepan. Add white onions; sauté 2 minutes. Pour in water and cook onions, covered, until just tender, about 12 minutes. Drain and set aside. Sauté mushrooms in 2 tablespoons butter and 1 tablespoon lemon juice for 5 minutes. Remove from heat and set aside. When veal is cooked, remove from stove and take out. Strain 2 cups of liquid and set aside. Melt 2 tablespoons butter in a large saucepan. Add flour and cook, stirring, 1 minute. Gradually add strained veal liquid and cook, stirring, until sauce is thickened and smooth. Combine egg yolks and cream; beat lightly. Mix a small amount of hot sauce with egg yolks. Return mixture to sauce. Cook slowly, stirring, until thickened. Season with salt, pepper, and nutmeg. Add reserved veal, onions, mushrooms and drippings, and remaining 1 tablespoon lemon juice. Leave on stove long enough to heat through. Serves 6.

Midwestern Sausage-Bean Ragout

This is an easy-to-prepare ragout for a family supper.

1 cup dried white beans, washed
2 medium-sized onions, peeled and chopped
2 cloves garlic, crushed
3 tablespoons bacon fat or shortening
1 can (1 pound) tomatoes, chopped
1 can (6 ounces) tomato paste
1 teaspoon dried rosemary or thyme
2 teaspoons salt
¼ teaspoon pepper
1 pound pork sausage links, fried, drained, and cut up
3 tablespoons chopped fresh parsley

Put beans in a large kettle. Cover with cold water; bring to a boil and boil 2 minutes. Remove from heat and let stand, covered, 1 hour. Meanwhile, sauté onions and garlic in heated fat or shortening in another large kettle. Add tomatoes, tomato paste, rosemary or thyme; mix well. Cook slowly, uncovered, 5 minutes. Add beans and water. Simmer, covered, 1½ hours, until beans are tender, adding more water, if needed. Season with salt and pepper. Mix in sausages 5 minutes before cooking is finished. Serve garnished with parsley. Serves 4.

Provençal Duckling Ragout

This delectable wine flavored ragout is an elegant entrée for a company dinner.

4 thin slices bacon, chopped

2 to 3 tablespoons salad oil
6 shallots or scallions, with some tops, minced
1 to 2 cloves garlic, crushed
2 ducklings, 4 to 5 pounds each, cut into serving pieces
3 tablespoons all-purpose flour
About 1½ cups dry red wine
1 cup beef bouillon
¼ cup tomato purée
⅓ cup brandy
1 bay leaf
3 sprigs parsley
½ teaspoon dried thyme
½ teaspoon crumbled dried rosemary
2 teaspoons salt
½ teaspoon pepper
24 small white onions, peeled
24 whole fresh mushrooms, cleaned

Cook bacon in a large kettle to render some of the fat. Add oil, shallots or scallions, and garlic; sauté 5 minutes. Wipe duckling pieces dry and fry, a few at a time, on all sides until golden. Spoon off any excess fat. Mix in flour and blend well. Add wine, bouillon, tomato purée, brandy, bay leaf, parsley, thyme, rosemary, salt, and pepper. Mix well and bring to a boil. Lower heat and cook slowly, covered, 1 hour. Add onions and continue to cook slowly about 30 minutes longer, until ducklings and onions are tender. Add mushrooms during last 10 minutes of cooking. Remove and discard bay leaf and parsley. Serves 8.

Austrian Chicken Ragout

This rich paprika flavored ragout includes sour cream and dill. It is a good entree for a special occasion luncheon.

> *2 broiler-fryer chickens, about 2½ pounds each, cut up*
> *Salt, pepper*
> *⅓ cup butter or margarine*
> *2 medium-sized onions, peeled and chopped*
> *2 tablespoons paprika, preferably Hungarian*
> *2 medium-sized tomatoes, peeled and chopped*
> *2 cups chicken broth*
> *2 tablespoons all-purpose flour*
> *2 cups sour cream at room temperature*
> *3 tablespoons chopped fresh dill*

Wipe chicken pieces dry with paper toweling. Sprinkle surfaces with salt and pepper. Brown in heated butter or margarine on all sides in a kettle. Remove to a plate and keep warm. Add onions to drippings; sauté until tender. Stir in paprika and cook 1 minute. Add tomatoes and chicken broth. Return chicken pieces to kettle. Cook slowly, covered, about 35 minutes, until chicken is tender. Remove chicken and keep warm. Scrape drippings and stir in flour. Gradually add sour cream and cook over low heat, stirring, until thickened and smooth. Spoon sauce over chicken and sprinkle with dill. Serves 6 to 8.

New Orleans Fish Ragout

This flavorful ragout is a good main dish for a Friday night supper.

> *1 large onion, peeled and chopped*
> *2 cloves garlic, crushed*
> *1 medium-sized green pepper, cleaned and chopped*
> *3 tablespoons salad oil*
> *1 can (1 pound) tomatoes, chopped*

1 *bay leaf*
1 *tablespoon Worcestershire sauce*
1 *teaspoon dried basil*
⅛ *teaspoon cayenne*
1½ *teaspoons salt*
½ *teaspoon pepper*
1 *cup uncooked long grain rice*
2 *cups chicken broth*
1 *pound flounder, red snapper, or red fish fillets, cubed*
3 *tablespoons chopped fresh parsley*

Sauté onion, garlic, and green pepper in heated oil in a large kettle 5 minutes. Add tomatoes, bay leaf, Worcestershire sauce, basil, cayenne, salt, and pepper. Cook slowly, uncovered, 5 minutes. Add rice and chicken broth. Cook slowly, covered, 25 minutes. Add fish cubes and cook about 15 minutes longer, until rice and fish are tender. Mix in parsley. Serves 4 to 6.

Bordeaux Beef Ragout

From the wine-rich region of Bordeaux in France comes this flavorful beef stew that is one of the best French ragouts. Serve for a company dinner.

3 *pounds beef sirloin, round, or chuck, cut into 2-inch*
cubes
¼ *cup all-purpose flour*
2 *teaspoons salt*
¼ *teaspoon pepper*
¼ *cup olive or salad oil*
¾ *cup minced scallions, with some tops*
1 *large clove garlic, crushed*
About 2 cups dry red wine

2 sprigs parsley
1 bay leaf
1 teaspoon dried thyme
*½ pound fresh mushrooms, cleaned and sliced
  lengthwise into halves*
1 can (1 pound) small white onions, drained

Wipe beef cubes dry with paper toweling. Dredge with flour, seasoned with salt and pepper. Brown in heated oil on all sides in a large saucepan. Remove to a plate. Add scallions and garlic; sauté 1 minute. Add wine, parsley, bay leaf, and thyme. Return beef to kettle; mix well. Bring to a boil and lower heat. Cook slowly, covered, about 1½ hours, until beef is tender. Add mushrooms and onions during last 10 minutes of cooking. Remove and discard parsley and bay leaf. Serves 8.

Electric

Slow-Cooker Dishes

Superb one-dish meals can be easily and economically prepared in modern attractive electric slow-cooking pots. All sorts of recipes lend themselves to the slow-cookery method and you can enjoy them all—from casseroles and curries to meat loaves and pot roasts.

The practice of cooking at a very low heat for a very long time in an earthenware pot is an ancient one. Our forefathers enjoyed meals from black iron kettles or skillets that simmered all day at the back of a wood-fueled stove. Electric utensils, created only a few years ago, are but modern adaptations of the old utensils and cooking customs.

The electric slow-cookers which have become popular in America and in some European countries have appealing advantages. Many of the preparation and cleaning chores are eliminated, and no steam escapes, keeping the kitchen from getting overheated or soiled. Since there is no need for pot watching or tending, you can fill the pot in the morning and relax at home for hours, or go out all day and return to a meal fully cooked. Furthermore, the constant low temperature costs only a few pennies a day. Slow-cookers are safe, take up little space, and most of them are suitable for serving at the table, if desired.

The long, slow cooking in electric pots produces delectable dishes that are notable for retaining and enhancing natural flavors. Inexpensive cuts of meats can be used in many cases, as the extended cooking process tenderizes them and brings out their finest qualities. You will find that even frankfurters and hamburgers benefit from slow-cookery.

It is possible to prepare your favorite international and family recipes in electric pots if they are adapted to the process. Consequently, many cooks prefer to use recipes that have been developed especially for the utensil until they understand the differing requirements of slow-cookery.

Choosing a slow-cooker is a personal matter, since there are many kinds. Each brand has a different design, capacity, shape, type of cord, and temperature settings. Basically, the cooker is an earthenware, stoneware, metal, ceramic or glass casserole or liner set into a metal utensil fitted with electric heating elements. As crockery is a term for several varieties of stoneware and earthenware, some utensils are called crockery pots. Well-fitted lids ensure heat retention.

All pots come with manufacturer's instructions, which should be carefully read and followed to learn about capacity, seasoning, and temperature scale, as well as cleaning and caring for the various surfaces. Pots with attached cords, for example, should not be immersed in water. Do not touch hot surfaces, and do use handles or knobs for moving the pots.

To get a better idea of the length of time proper slow-cooking will require, you should understand that the contents of slow-cookers are slowly heated to a simmering point and remain at the temperature marked "low" (190°F.–200°F.) or "high"

(300°F.) for as long as the utensil is operating. Low is the best temperature for most cooking. Some foods, however, are cooked partially on high, which may be used to accelerate the cooking time if you are in a hurry. Start a soup, for example, on high for three hours and then finish it on low.

You cannot overlook or burn foods in a slow-cooker, and it doesn't matter if the ingredients cook even two hours or so longer than the recipe specifies. But it is possible to undercook foods so be sure to allow sufficient time.

Cooking times cannot be compared to those for conventional stoves because of the unique heating systems, low temperatures, and long cooking periods. Consequently, recipes for slow-cooking cannot be specific about cooking time. Generally, equate 20 to 30 minutes of conventional cooking time to four to eight hours at low and 1½ to 2½ hours at high. One hour of high is equal to 2½ hours on low.

It is not necessary to stir a majority of the dishes while cooking in the pots. Do not uncover the dishes while cooking unless absolutely necessary as removing the lid results in losing steam and reducing the temperature. Each time the lid is taken off an additional 15 to 20 minutes of cooking time will be required.

Follow these guidelines when you're preparing foods for slow-cookers. Meats should be trimmed of any fat or browned to remove all excess fat before putting into the pot. Larger cuts of meat require longer cooking than ground or cubed meat. Wipe meats and poultry dry before cooking.

Some vegetables, especially root vegetables, take longer to cook than meats, so it's best to cut them into small pieces and put them into the pot underneath the meat so that they are nearer the direct heat.

Slowly cooked dishes require less liquid than conventional recipes because the juices of the meats and vegetables are not boiled away. When adapting a conventional recipe, use half the amount of liquid. Any excess juices can be reduced at the end of the cooking by removing the cover and cooking on high about 45 minutes.

Be careful with seasonings for these dishes because the slow-cooker method enhances flavors. Use smaller amounts of spices and herbs. Dairy products such as milk, cream, sour cream, or yogurt should be added to the dish during the last hour of cooking, because prolonged cooking may cause them to curdle.

The following American and international dishes have been adapted for slow-cooking and are designed for a 3½-quart pot. You will find that they are not only convenient to prepare but add interest to family and company meals.

French Onion Soup

This is a good and hearty soup for a late supper.

4 large onions, peeled and sliced
⅓ cup butter or margarine
8 cups beef bouillon
1½ teaspoons salt
½ teaspoon pepper
Freshly grated nutmeg to taste
1 cup grated Parmesan cheese
6 to 8 slices toasted French bread

Separate onions and sauté in heated butter or margarine in a large skillet until tender. Spoon into bottom of slow-cooking pot. Add bouillon, salt, and pepper. Cook, covered, on low 6 to 8 hours. Stir in nutmeg and grated cheese. Serve in large bowls over toasted bread. Serves 6 to 8.

German Ham-Lentil Soup

Serve for a winter supper or luncheon.

1 pound (2 cups) lentils
1 large onion, peeled and minced
2 cloves garlic, crushed
2 large carrots, scraped and minced
2 large stalks celery, with leaves, cleaned and chopped
1 can (1 pound) tomatoes, chopped
7 cups water
1 teaspoon dried thyme
1½ teaspoons salt
½ teaspoon pepper
1 package (10 ounces) frozen chopped spinach, partially
   defrosted
2 cups diced smoked ham

Soak lentils in cold water to cover overnight. Drain. Put with other ingredients, except spinach and ham, in slow-cooking pot. Cook on low, covered, 8 to 10 hours. Add spinach and ham during last hour of cooking. Serves 8 to 10.

Canadian Sausage-Split Pea Soup

This is an appealing soup for a family dinner.

1 pound dry green split peas
1 large onion, peeled and chopped
2 medium-sized carrots, scraped and diced
2 stalks celery, with leaves, cleaned and chopped
2 bay leaves

½ *teaspoon celery salt*
1 *teaspoon salt*
¼ *teaspoon pepper*
1 *pound bulk sausage*

Soak green peas in water to cover overnight. Drain, reserving water. Add enough water to make 7 cups. Put green peas, water, and remaining ingredients, except sausage, in slow-cooking pot. Cook on low, covered, 8 to 10 hours. Meanwhile, fry sausage, mincing with a fork, until redness disappears. Drain off all fat. Add to soup two hours after it has been cooking. Serves 8 to 10.

Old-Fashioned Chicken-Vegetable Soup

You'll enjoy this favorite soup for a weekend luncheon or supper.

1 *large onion, peeled and chopped*
2 *large stalks celery, with leaves, cleaned and sliced*
1 *can (12 ounces) whole kernel corn, drained*
1 *can (1 pound, 12 ounces) tomatoes, chopped*
3 *cups diced cooked chicken (or turkey)*
1 *can (6 ounces) tomato paste*
6 *cups chicken broth*
2 *teaspoons parsley flakes*
1 *teaspoon dried marjoram*
1 *tablespoon Worcestershire sauce*
1½ *teaspoons salt*
½ *teaspoon pepper*

Put all ingredients in slow-cooking pot. Cook on low, covered, 6 to 8 hours. Serves 10 to 12.

Down East Fish Chowder

A good dish for a company luncheon or supper.

> *2 pounds fresh or frozen cod or haddock fillets, cut into*
>   *1-inch pieces*
> *¼ pound salt pork, diced*
> *2 large onions, peeled and chopped*
> *4 cups diced peeled raw potatoes*
> *4 cups hot water*
> *1½ teaspoons salt*
> *1 cup light cream or milk, scalded*
> *1 tablespoon butter or margarine*
> *¼ teaspoon pepper*
> *6 large soda crackers, split in half, or 6 slices toasted*
>   *crusty white bread*

If frozen fillets are used, thaw them. Fry salt pork in a small skillet; add onions and sauté until tender. Spoon into bottom of slow-cooking pot. Add fish pieces, potatoes, water, and salt. Cook on low, covered, 6 to 8 hours, until potatoes are tender. Add cream or milk, butter or margarine, and pepper during last hour of cooking. Serve in large bowls over crackers or toast. Serves 6.

Provençal Chicken with Zucchini

This is an attractive and delectable entrée for a summer luncheon.

> *1 large onion, peeled and sliced*

2 cloves garlic, minced
1 broiler-fryer chicken, about 2½ pounds, cut up
1 can (1 pound) whole tomatoes, chopped
½ cup dry white wine or chicken broth
1 bay leaf
1 teaspoon dried thyme
1½ teaspoons salt
¼ teaspoon pepper
1 bag (1 pound, 4 ounces) frozen zucchini slices,
*   partially defrosted*

Put onion and garlic in bottom of slow-cooking pot. Wash chicken pieces and wipe dry. Place over onions. Add remaining ingredients, except zucchini. Cook on low, covered, 6 to 8 hours. Add zucchini during last hour of cooking. Serves 4 to 6.

Pot Roast, Italian Style

This flavorful beef roast, cooked with vegetables, is an appealing entrée for a family dinner.

1 4- to 4½-pound boneless beef pot roast
1 large onion, peeled and sliced
2 cloves garlic, crushed
2 medium-sized green peppers, cleaned and sliced
4 whole fresh or canned tomatoes, drained and chopped
½ cup liquid from canned tomatoes or tomato juice
1½ teaspoons salt
½ teaspoon pepper
1 teaspoon dried oregano
½ teaspoon dried basil

Cut off and discard any excess fat from pot roast. Wipe dry.

Put onion, garlic, green peppers, tomatoes, tomato liquid or tomato juice, salt, and pepper in bottom of slow-cooking pot. Place beef over ingredients. Cook, covered, on low 10 to 12 hours. Add oregano and basil during last hour of cooking. Serve sliced topped with vegetables and sauce. Serves 8.

Southern Barbecued Chicken

This is an old favorite that is good for a summer supper or luncheon.

> *1 broiler-fryer chicken, about 2½ pounds, cut up*
> *½ cup catsup*
> *¼ cup cider vinegar*
> *2 tablespoons molasses*
> *1 tablespoon Worcestershire sauce*
> *1 tablespoon brown sugar*
> *1 tablespoon instant onion*
> *Few drops Tabasco sauce*
> *1 teaspoon salt*
> *¼ teaspoon pepper*

Wash chicken quarters and dry. Put in bottom of slow-cooking pot. Combine remaining ingredients and pour over chicken. Cook on low, covered, 6 to 8 hours. Serves 4.

Meat Loaf, Mexican Style

An interesting meat loaf for a buffet dinner.

> *2 pounds meat loaf mixture (beef, veal and pork) or lean*
> *ground beef*

1 cup fine dry breadcrumbs
½ cup milk or beef bouillon
1 medium-sized onion, peeled and minced
2 eggs, beaten
1 teaspoon dried oregano
2 teaspoons parsley flakes
1½ teaspoons salt
¼ teaspoon pepper
1 large green pepper, cleaned and chopped
2 large tomatoes, peeled and chopped
1 can (12 ounces) whole kernel corn, drained

Combine meat loaf mixture or beef with bread crumbs, milk or bouillon, onion, eggs, oregano, parsley flakes, salt, and pepper in a large bowl. Shape into a round loaf. Put green peppers, tomatoes, and corn in bottom of slow-cooking pot. Place meat loaf over vegetables. Cook on low, covered, 8 to 10 hours. While cooking, spoon off any accumulated fat on top of meat loaf. Do this only once or twice. Serve sliced and topped and surrounded with vegetables. Serves 8.

Italian Meatball-Vegetable Stew

All the family will enjoy this entree for a dinner.

2 pounds lean ground beef
¾ cup fine dry bread crumbs
½ cup tomato juice or milk
2 eggs
1 teaspoon dried oregano
1½ teaspoons salt
½ teaspoon pepper
3 medium-sized onions, peeled and quartered

3 large carrots, scraped and cut into 1-inch slices
1 can (1 pound) tomatoes, chopped
1 package (10 ounces) frozen cut-up green beans,
  partially defrosted
3 tablespoons chopped fresh parsley

Combine beef, bread crumbs, tomato juice or milk, eggs, oregano, salt, and pepper in a large bowl. Form into 2-inch balls. Put onions and carrots in bottom of slow-cooking pot. Arrange meatballs over them. Cook on low, covered, 4 to 6 hours. Turn to high. Add green beans and parsley and cook 40 minutes longer. Serves 8.

Italian Spaghetti with Meat Sauce

Serve this flavorful spaghetti specialty for a family supper.

2 pounds lean ground beef
2 large onions, peeled and chopped
2 cloves garlic, minced
1 can (1 pound, 12 ounces) tomatoes, chopped
2 cans (6 ounces each) tomato paste
½ cup beef bouillon
1½ teaspoons dried oregano
1 teaspoon dried basil
1 tablespoon parsley flakes
1½ teaspoons salt
¼ teaspoon pepper
1 pound thin spaghetti, cooked and drained

Brown beef, mixing with a fork, in a large skillet until redness disappears. Pour off all accumulated fat. Combine beef with remaining ingredients, except spaghetti, in slow-cooking pot.

Cook on low, covered, 8 to 10 hours. Serve over hot spaghetti. Serves 8.

Chili Con Carne

This well-known specialty is a good supper entrée.

1 pound lean ground beef
1 large onion, peeled end chopped
1 large green pepper, cleaned and chopped
2 cloves garlic, crushed
1 can (1 pound) tomatoes, chopped
1 can (1 pound) kidney beans, drained
2 to 3 tablespoons chili powder
1 bay leaf
1 teaspoon dried oregano
1 teaspoon salt
¼ teaspoon pepper

Brown beef, mixing with a fork, in a large skillet until redness disappears. Pour off all fat. Combine beef with other ingredients in a slow-cooking pot. Cook on low, covered, 6 to 8 hours. Remove and discard bay leaf. Serves 6.

Turkish Lamb-Vegetable Stew

This is an appealing entree for a company dinner.

1½ pounds boneless lamb, cut into 1½-inch cubes
1 tablespoon salad oil
1 medium-sized eggplant, stemmed, cubed and parboiled

2 medium-sized zucchini, stemmed and sliced
1 large onion, peeled and sliced
2 cloves garlic, crushed
3 medium-sized tomatoes, peeled and chopped
1 teaspoon dried oregano or thyme
1½ teaspoons salt
½ teaspoon pepper
1 package (10 ounces) frozen cut-up green beans,
partially defrosted

Brown lamb in heated oil in a large skillet. Remove with a slotted spoon to a plate. Put eggplant, zucchini, onion, garlic, and tomatoes in bottom of slow-cooking pot. Top with lamb cubes, oregano or thyme, salt, and pepper. Cook on low, covered, 8 to 10 hours. Turn to high. Add green beans and cook another 40 minutes, until ingredients are tender. Serves 6.

Jewish Sweet-Sour Meatballs

This is a flavorful entree for a company late evening meal.

2 pounds lean ground beef
¾ cup fine dry breadcrumbs
½ cup milk
2 eggs
¼ cup chopped fresh mint or parsley
1½ teaspoons salt
½ teaspoon pepper
1 large onion, peeled and chopped
1 large green pepper, cleaned and cubed
1 can (6 ounces) tomato paste
1 cup beef bouillon

Juice of 1 lemon
⅓ cup brown sugar
⅓ cup currants or seedless raisins

Combine beef, breadcrumbs, milk, eggs, mint or parsley, salt, and pepper in a large bowl. Form into 2-inch balls. Put onion and green pepper in bottom of slow-cooking pot. Arrange meatballs over them. Add remaining ingredients. Cook on low, covered, 8 to 10 hours. Serves 8.

Easy Turkey-Potato Casserole

You can prepare this casserole with leftover cooked turkey for a family supper.

3 cups cubed cooked turkey
3 medium-sized raw potatoes, peeled and chopped
1 cup diced celery
1 cup diced green pepper
1 cup tomato sauce
1 tablespoon Worcestershire sauce
2 teaspoons parsley flakes
1 teaspoon dried marjoram
1 teaspoon salt
¼ teaspoon pepper

Combine all ingredients in a large bowl. Turn into slow-cooking pot. Cook on high, covered, 2 hours. Reduce heat to low and cook 4 to 6 hours longer. Serves 6 to 8.

Provençal Cod Fillets

A good entrée for a summer luncheon or supper.

1 pound fresh or frozen cod fillets
1 large onion, peeled and sliced
2 cloves garlic, crushed
2 tomatoes, peeled and chopped
2 small zucchini, stemmed and sliced
½ cup dry white wine
2 tablespoons lemon juice
1 teaspoon dried oregano or thyme
1½ teaspoons salt
½ teaspoon pepper
6 stuffed green olives, sliced

If frozen cod fillets are used, thaw them. Put onion, garlic, tomatoes and zucchini in bottom of slow cooking pot. Place cod fillets over them. Add remaining ingredients. Cook on low, covered, 8 to 10 hours. Serves 4 to 6.

Curried Bean-Hamburger Pot

This easy-to-prepare pot is an inexpensive entrée for a late evening party or family supper.

1 pound dried beans, navy, red or kidney
6 cups water
1½ pounds lean ground beef
1 tablespoon ground turmeric
1 tablespoon chili powder
1 teaspoon ground cumin or coriander

1 can (1 pound, 12 ounces) tomatoes, chopped
2 tablespoons Worcestershire sauce
1½ teaspoons salt
½ teaspoon pepper

Soak beans in water overnight. Put into slow-cooking pot and cook, covered, on high 2 to 3 hours, until tender. Drain. Meanwhile, brown beef in a large skillet, stirring with a fork, until redness disappears. Pour off any fat. Put beans, beef, and remaining ingredients into a slow-cooking pot. Cook, covered, on low 10 to 12 hours. Serves 8 to 10.

Greek Island Fish Stew

You'll enjoy this tomato and herb flavored fish specialty for a weekend luncheon.

2 pounds fresh or frozen white-fleshed fish fillets (cod,
*   flounder, haddock)*
2 large onions, peeled and sliced
2 or 3 garlic cloves, crushed
4 whole fresh or canned tomatoes, peeled and chopped
½ cup fish broth or water
1 bay leaf
1 teaspoon dried oregano or thyme
1 teaspoon salt
¼ teaspoon pepper
3 tablespoons chopped fresh parsley

If frozen fish fillets are used, thaw them. Cut fresh or frozen fillets into bite-size pieces. Put onions, garlic, and tomatoes in bottom of slow-cooking pot. Arrange fish pieces over them. Add remaining ingredients. Cook on low, covered, 6 to 8 hours. Serve in large bowls over toasted crusty white bread, if desired. Serves 6.

Spanish Meat Loaf with Vegetables

This meat loaf, cooked with eggplant, green peppers and tomatoes, is an attractive entrée for a company dinner.

2 pounds lean ground beef
1 cup seasoned breadcrumbs
½ cup tomato juice
1 medium-sized onion, peeled and minced
2 eggs
1 teaspoon dried thyme
1½ teaspoons salt
½ teaspoon pepper
1 medium-sized eggplant, stemmed, cubed and parboiled
1 large green pepper, cleaned and cubed
1 can (1 pound) tomatoes, chopped

Combine beef, breadcrumbs, tomato juice, onion, eggs. thyme, salt, and pepper in a large bowl. Shape into a round loaf. Put eggplant, green pepper, and tomatoes in bottom of slow-cooking pot. Place meat loaf over vegetables. Cook on low, covered, 8 to 10 hours. While cooking, spoon off any accumulated fat on top of meat loaf. Do this only once or twice. Serve sliced and topped and surrounded with vegetables. Serves 8.

French Chicken in a Pot

This flavorful chicken-rice dish is a good entrée for an informal weekend dinner.

1 large onion, peeled and sliced
2 cloves garlic, crushed
2 large carrots, scraped and diced
2 large stalks celery, with leaves, cleaned and sliced
1 broiler-fryer chicken, about 2½ pounds, cut up
1 cup dry white wine or chicken broth
1 teaspoon crumbled dried rosemary
1½ teaspoons salt
½ teaspoon pepper
3 cups cooked long grain rice
½ cup chopped fresh parsley

Put onion, garlic, carrots, and celery in bottom of slow-cooking pot. Wash and wipe dry chicken pieces. Place over vegetables. Add wine or chicken broth, rosemary, salt, and pepper. Cook on low, covered, 6 to 8 hours. Add rice and parsley during last hour of cooking. Serves 6.

German Frankfurter-Sauerkraut Pot

This is a hearty entrée for a winter dinner.

1 large onion, peeled and chopped
1 large green pepper, cleaned and chopped
1 tart apple, peeled, cored and chopped
1 can (1 pound) sauerkraut, drained
⅛ teaspoon celery seeds

1 teaspoon dried thyme
1 teaspoon salt
½ teaspoon pepper
1 pound frankfurters
⅓ cup tomato juice
1 cup sour cream at room temperature
¼ cup chopped fresh parsley

Put onion, green pepper, apple, sauerkraut, celery seeds, thyme, salt, and pepper in bottom of slow-cooking pot. Place frankfurters over vegetables and apple. Add tomato juice. Cook on low, covered, 6 to 8 hours. Add sour cream and parsley during last hour of cooking. Serves 4 to 6.

Russian Beef Stroganoff

This elegant entrée is excellent for a company dinner.

2 pounds round or flank steak
1 large onion, peeled and chopped
3 tablespoons tomato paste
1 tablespoon prepared mustard
½ cup beef bouillon
1½ teaspoons salt
½ teaspoon pepper
½ pound fresh mushrooms, cleaned and sliced
1 tablespoon all-purpose flour
1 cup sour cream at room temperature

Remove and discard any fat from steak. Cut at a slant into strips about ½ inch thick and 3 inches long. Put onion in bottom of slow-cooking pot. Place steak strips over onion. Combine tomato paste, mustard, bouillon, salt, and pepper. Pour over steak. Cook on low, covered, 6 to 8 hours. Add mushrooms and flour, mixed with sour cream, during last hour of cooking. Serves 4.

Texas Franks with Chili Sauce

Serve these flavorful frankfurters for an informal supper or outdoor meal.

1 medium-sized onion, peeled and minced
1 medium-sized green pepper, cleaned and minced
2 cloves garlic, crushed
1 cup catsup
¼ cup cider vinegar
2 tablespoons Worcestershire sauce
2 tablespoons salad oil
1 teaspoon salt
¼ teaspoon pepper
Few drops hot sauce
1 pound frankfurters, cut into 1-inch slices

Put all ingredients, except frankfurter slices, in bottom of slow-cooking pot. Place frankfurter slices over ingredients. Cook on low, covered, 6 to 8 hours. Serves 4.

Coq au Vin

This well-known French specialty, chicken in wine, is an elegant entrée for a company luncheon or dinner.

1 fryer-broiler chicken, about 2½ pounds, cut up
¼ cup butter or margarine
2 tablespoons olive or salad oil
2 slices bacon, chopped
1½ small white onions, peeled
½ pound whole fresh mushrooms, cleaned
2 garlic cloves, crushed
1 teaspoon dried thyme
1 teaspoon salt
¼ teaspoon pepper
¼ cup brandy
3 tablespoons chopped fresh parsley

Wash chicken pieces and wipe dry. Heat butter or margarine, oil, and bacon in a large skillet. Add chicken pieces and fry until golden on all sides. Remove from heat. Add onions and sauté in drippings until golden. Put onions with drippings, mushrooms, and garlic in bottom of slow-cooking pot. Place chicken pieces over them. Add thyme, salt, pepper, and red wine. Cook on low, covered, 6 to 8 hours. Add brandy and parsley during last hour of cooking. Serves 4 to 6.

Irish Stew

You will enjoy this well-known entrée for a family dinner.

2 pounds boneless lamb shoulder or breast, cut into 2-inch cubes
2 medium-sized onions, peeled and chopped
2 medium-sized carrots, scraped and sliced
3 medium-sized potatoes, peeled and sliced
½ teaspoon dried thyme

3 tablespoons chopped fresh parsley
1 teaspoon salt
¼ teaspoon pepper
2 cups water

Arrange lamb cubes and vegetables in layers in slow-cooking pot. Add remaining ingredients. Cook at low, covered, 10 to 12 hours.

Metric Measure Conversion Table
(Approximations)

When You Know (U.S.)	Multiply by	To Find (Metric)
WEIGHT		
ounces	28	grams
pounds	0.45	kilograms
VOLUME		
teaspoons	5	milliliters
tablespoons	15	milliliters
fluid ounces	30	milliliters
cups	0.24	liters
pints	0.47	liters
quarts	0.95	liters
TEMPERATURE		
degrees Fahrenheit (°F)	subtract 32° and multiply the remainder by 5/9 or .556	degrees Celsius or Centigrade (°C)

Index